MAKING SENSE

Teaching and Learning Mathematics with Understanding

James Hiebert

Thomas P. Carpenter

Elizabeth Fennema

Karen C. Fuson

Diana Wearne

Hanlie Murray

Alwyn Olivier

Piet Human

Foreword by Mary M. Lindquist

HEINEMANN
Portsmouth, NH

HEINEMANN
A division of Reed Elsevier Inc.
361 Hanover Street
Portsmouth, NH 03801–3912

Offices and agents throughout the world

The authors and publisher wish to thank those who have generously
given permission to reprint borrowed material:

Figure 8–2, from *McDonald's Nutrition Facts*. Copyright © 1996. Reprinted
by permission of McDonald's Corporation.

Library of Congress Cataloging-in-Publication Data

Making sense : teaching and learning mathematics with understanding /
  James Hiebert . . . [et al.] ; foreword by Mary M. Lindquist.
      p.   cm.
    Includes bibliographical references.
    ISBN 0-435-07132-7
    1. Mathematics—Study and teaching (Elementary)—United States.
  2. Mathematics—Study and teaching (Elementary)—United States—Case
  studies.   I. Hiebert, James.
  QA135.5.M335   1997
  372.7'044—dc21   97-1960
                                                                    CIP

Editor: Leigh Peake
Production: Vicki Kasabian
Cover design: Michael Leary
Manufacturing: Louise Richardson

Printed in the United States of America on acid-free paper
03 02   EB   11

Contents

Foreword

Almost all, who have ever fully understood arithmetic, have been obliged to learn it over again in their own way.

Warren Colburn

When I read old arithmetic textbooks such as Colburn's, I wonder what would have happened if we had listened to the advice of those who, through the ages, have recommended that mathematics should make sense to students. The tiny book of Colburn was hailed as the most valuable school book in the country. One user testified, "I find that those children introduced to arithmetic by it, have a clearer *understanding* of the operations than those who use any other introduction whatever. I believe that the universal adoption of it as elementary work would increase the intelligence of all the children in the country" (Colburn 1849, back cover, emphasis added).

Although it was a popular text, I doubt if the author's claims, made in the key to a later edition of the text, were realized:

> Instructers [*sic*] who may never have attended to fractions need not be afraid to undertake to teach this book. The author flatters himself that the principles are so illustrated and the processes are made so simple, that any one, who shall undertake to teach it, will find himself familiar with fractions before he is aware of it, although he knewth nothing of them before; and that every one will acquire a facility in solving questions which he never before possessed. (Colburn 1849, 141)

We still have students and teachers who have not developed those understandings and, furthermore, some who do not believe that they can or need to develop understanding. We all have listened to students who have come to believe that mathematics does not need to make sense. Recently, a teacher in one of my classes interviewed her students about proportional statements taken from Lamon (1995). One sixth-grade student was asked whether the statement "if one girl has three brothers, then two girls have six brothers" made sense. The student responded, "It really does not make much sense. But, we are in math class, so I guess it does in here." During one of my first years of teaching, one of my most capable students said, "In math, I do things just the opposite way from what I think they should be, and it almost always works." She was referring to the rule about a positive second derivative indicating a possible minimum, but she cited many more of her interpretations of these "nonsense" rules.

Why do we worry about making sense or understanding what we are doing? The sixth-grade student was receiving good grades, as was my college student. If we turn to the wisdom of the past, we gain much insight about understanding. The operational definition of understanding may have changed, but often the reasons given for helping students develop understanding are just as applicable today as in the past. After briefly touching on perspectives from history, we will return to the question of why we have not made more progress, and to thoughts about what this book may contribute to the pursuit of learning with understanding.

What Can We Learn from the Past About Understanding?

Throughout this century psychologists, educators, and others have been concerned with understanding. I have selected only a few of those who focused on learning relevant to mathematics to illustrate the changing views of and emphases on understanding. In their works, often interspersed in the ebb and flow of attention to understanding, we see different views of understanding and recommendations for learning with understanding.

Early in the Century

Thorndike, in psychology, and Dewey, in philosophy, both influenced education in the beginning third of this century. Dewey cautioned that the practice of teaching without understanding damaged students' ability to reflect and to make sense of what they were doing:

> Sheer imitation, dictation of steps to be taken, mechanical drills may give results most quickly and yet strengthen traits likely to be fatal to reflective power. The pupil is enjoined to do this and that specific thing, with no knowledge of any reason except that by so doing he gets his result most speedily; his mistakes are pointed out and corrected for him, he is kept at pure repetition of certain acts till they become automatic.

Later, teachers wonder why the pupil reads with so little expression, and figures with so little intelligent consideration of the terms of his problem. (Dewey 1910, 51–52)

For Dewey, learning was problem solving that depended upon an individual's aims and interests. He saw the learning as emerging from experiences or problem-solving activities. The role of the teacher was to provide these experiences for the individual.

This view of learning was often contrasted and often credited with the downfall of Thorndike's connectionism. However, reaction to the progressive movement, especially the misinterpretations of incidental learning, prodded the education community to return to what more closely resembled Thorndike's principles of learning. We entered a period in which there was more emphasis on drill of small, isolated facts—exactly what Dewey was cautioning against.

The Thirties, Forties, and Early Fifties

As the pendulum continued to swing toward a more mechanistic learning, Brownell provided an alternate force as he wrote about meaningful learning:

According to the *meaning* theory, the ultimate purpose of arithmetic instruction is the development of the ability to *think* in quantitative situations. The word "think" is used advisedly: the ability merely to perform certain operations mechanically and automatically is not enough. Children must be able to analyze real or described quantitative situations. (Brownell 1935, 28)

During the next twenty years, much of Brownell's research centered on learning with meaning and he proposed the following ten reasons to develop meaning as a student learned:

1. gives assurance of retention

2. equips him with the means to rehabilitate quickly skills that are temporarily weak

3. increases the likelihood that arithmetical ideas and skills will be used

4. contributes to ease of learning by providing a sound foundation and transferable understandings

5. reduces the amount of repetitive practice necessary to complete learning

6. safeguards him from answers that are mathematically absurd

7. encourages learning by problem solving in place of unintelligent memorization and practice

8. provides him with a versatility of attack which enables him to substitute equally effective procedures for procedures normally used but not available at the time

9. makes him relatively independent so that he faces new quantitative situations with confidence

10. presents the subject in a way which makes it worthy of respect (Brownell 1947, 263–64)

One of the strongest but least known advocates for meaning theory during this time was Wheat. In his book, *Psychology and Teaching of Arithmetic* (1937, iii), he disputed a prevalent interpretation of incidentalist beliefs that "arithmetic was part of the material world in which children live, and that it may be extracted by them in proportion to their contacts with the material world." His book also challenged the learning of separate number facts and called for learning about number ideas and relationships (185).

His comparison of learning arithmetic to taking a trip addresses both the role of the student and the role of the teacher:

> The pupil learns the way to think about the numbers of things that we call arithmetic as he explores the way. He learns the road of thinking and how to move along it as he travels the road. The speed of his movement is of minor importance as compared with the fact that, to progress, the pupil travels under his own power.
>
> In the case of the tourist, we map the route he should take and we point it out to him. In the case of the pupil, his teacher must do the same thing. While he is yet unable to recognize number questions, his teacher must point them out and make them clear. While he is yet untrained in the art of finding answers, his teacher must make clear what the finding of answers requires. His teacher must make clear what the pupil must look for and observe as he starts the unexplored part of his intellectual journey, at one place, then another along the road of number-thinking. Since his journey is intellectual, its nature and extent are determined by the objects of his attention and the ways he attends to them. (Wheat 1951, 25, 27)

Near the end of this time there was much discussion of what was meant by meaning. Van Engen (1947), in describing the development of meaning from the 1920s to the early 1940s, remarked that even Thorndike's writings indicated support of meaning but they never clearly addressed what meaning meant. In response to the lack of definition of meaning, many of Van Engen's writings addressed this need.

Van Engen urged that "any definition of meaning should enable the teacher to abstract from each experience those specific elements which develop mathematical meanings" (64). Van Engen's quote of Einstein, "If you want to know what I mean, don't listen to what I say, but watch what I do" exemplified his own message to teachers about how to develop meaning. In summary, he recommended the following: Show the students (or let them perform) the actions implied by operations on objects. As you talk, do not expect the students to learn without observing the actions on the objects. Then help students symbolize the actions, and later generalize to larger numbers for which the actions on objects become awkward. At this stage the structure of mathematics, or the generalization of the operation, should allow the student to work symbolically.

New Math and Back to Basics

Even in Van Engen's early work we begin to see influences that would be present in the "new math" movement. Meaning of school mathematics in the modern mathematics era was derived more from the structure of mathematics than it had been previously. We can also see residues of Brownell's reasons for developing meaning in the principles put forth by Bruner (1960). He urged that the learning of mathematics should be based on the understanding of fundamentals in a structured pattern. This would ensure that details be less rapidly forgotten and when forgotten they could be more easily reconstructed when needed. He also built the case that such learning would facilitate transfer.

The behaviorist approach that was present during the new mathematics time was embraced by those who returned to the so-called basics. In the era of behavioral objectives, we heard less about meaning, thinking, and understanding partly because they were difficult to measure. If we wrote an objective stating that students should understand, we were in deep trouble. Yet even in this time, many people were still studying and struggling with the ideas of understanding. Skemp helped practitioners to consider understanding from two perspectives. In a classic article in 1976 (reprinted in Skemp 1987), he defined *relational understanding* as knowing what to do and why and *instrumental understanding* as knowing what to do or the possession of a rule and ability to use it. For example, students say, "Oh, I understand" when they remember the next step in an algorithm (instrumental understanding). And, often students rebel when we try to show them why something works (our attempt to develop relational understanding). Skemp pointed to the difficulty of communicating using the term understanding if the sender is thinking of relational understanding and the receiver is thinking of instrumental understanding. This is especially relevant in the situation in which a teacher is teaching for relational understanding and a student is desiring instrumental understanding, or vice versa.

Skemp described some of the often-cited benefits of instrumental understanding, such as the rewards are more immediate and more apparent, and correct answers can be gotten more quickly. He then enumerated reasons for developing relational understanding. Relational understanding is more adaptable to new tasks and easier to remember. Relational knowledge is an effective goal in of itself because the need for rewards and punishments is greatly reduced. Relational schemas are organic in quality because they act as their own agents of change (Skemp 1987).

Today

In the 1980s, as psychologists and researchers in mathematics education were again studying understanding, the mathematics community was setting standards for what students should know and be able to do. One of the publications that helped set the stage for the need for standards was *Everybody Counts*. In this document, mathematics is described in a manner that called for understanding:

> Mathematics reveals hidden patterns that help us understand the world around us. . . .Mathematics is a science of pattern and order. . . .Its domain is . . . numbers, chance, form, algorithms, and change. . . . Mathematics relies on logic rather than on observation as its standard of truth, yet employs observation, simulation, and even experimentation as means of discovering truth. (National Research Council 1989, 31)

The *Standards* (National Council of Teachers of Mathematics 1989, 1991, 1995) emphasize the need for understanding in learning, teaching, and assessing mathematics. As important, the entire standards-based reform movement in schooling is described as one whose "focus [is] more on depth of understanding—how well students can reason with and use what they have learned—rather than on regurgitation of isolated facts." (McLaughlin, Shepard, and Day 1995, 9) Likewise, it is important that there is recognition beyond school mathematics for the need for understanding. As one collegiate mathematician recently stated, "large amounts of mathematics can be learned as sensible answers to sensible questions—that is, as part of mathematical sense making, rather than by 'mastery' of bits and pieces of knowledge" (Schoenfeld 1994, 59).

Why So Little Progress?

Tracing some of the writings of those who espoused understanding clearly points to the constant revisiting of this issue. Why, then, has learning with understanding not become part of our ethos?

I find the reasons why we should help students learn with understanding the most compelling part of the historical record. Even the brief quote of Colburn that opens this foreword causes me to pause and reflect on how and when I have gained understanding of mathematical ideas. I find the reasons of Brownell and Bruner for developing understanding to be consonant with my own learning experience and with evidence from my own teaching. They seem reasonable and sound; I am willing to make them part of my guiding principles. Yet, I still have many questions about my own teaching and the broader issues of reform.

Throughout the threads of the historical perspective you can feel the tension caused by the lack of clarity of what was meant by understanding. At times, advocates of understanding, such as Van Engen and Skemp, addressed directly this lack of clarity. At other times, there appeared to be an underlying assumption that we understood what we meant by understanding, meaning, or thinking. It is instructive to contrast the reasons given for developing understanding using an instrumental rather than a relational view of understanding. Although we have made progress on this issue, and this book will help us wrestle with what is meant by understanding, most of us have not completely resolved this issue. Pause for a minute and ask yourself what you mean by understanding. Then ask, how do you know when your students understand? What connections do you look for? What communication do you expect?

Has it only been this lack of definition or clarity of what is meant by understanding that has impeded our progress? I think not. There are many other influences that we need to consider to understand why we have lacked progress in the past and how we can make progress now.

Psychology

The prevalent psychological views during each of the periods were not always consonant with developing understanding. The contrasting views of Thorndike and Dewey—although each important to the later developing theories of psychology—may have prevented the moving forward of Dewey's view that is more closely aligned with developing understanding. Interpretations of behavioral psychology led us away from encouraging learning with understanding. Perhaps even more important, the prevalent psychology of learning was often not tied closely with a theory of teaching.

Mathematics

The prevailing view of school mathematics is one of rules and procedures, memorization and practice, and exactness in procedures and in answers. Many adults separate school mathematics, except for basic number ideas and skills, from the mathematics used in everyday life. There is no doubt that there are rules, need for practice, and exact answers. There is a need to store facts and procedures in memory. There are interesting mathematical problems that do not arise from a contextual or applied situation.

If mathematics is considered only as isolated facts and skills, then there is little use to encourage understanding. If mathematics is considered only as rules we memorize and practice, then thinking about these may be considered a waste of time. If mathematics is something we do only in school, then there is little point in developing a sense of when and how to apply mathematics. Through the years different slants on these views of mathematics have not lent themselves to encouraging a mathematics that makes sense.

Mathematical Learning

Our view of mathematical learning influences how we think about teaching. If we believe that education is mainly learning facts and procedures quickly and efficiently, if we believe that only certain students need or can learn mathematics, or if we believe that people are born with the ability to do or not to do mathematics, then our view will conflict with the development of understanding. If we look back in history, we see evidence for the first of these—educators during the time of Thorndike emphasized learning bits and pieces in an efficient manner. With regard to the second, it is only recently that we have moved from thinking of mathematics as an elite subject to one that is essential for all citizens. Finally, it is common in the United States for people to accept the ability argument, thus excusing many for not learning mathematics.

Educational Reform

Often we have had a view that educational problems can be fixed by changing one aspect, such as the curriculum, preparation of teachers, or assessment. For example, in the modern mathematics era, the focus mainly was on curriculum. Moving to classrooms that encourage understanding requires more than fiddling with one aspect, or adding more on to what is being done. It requires more substantive, long-term changes. It also requires a change in attitude and beliefs as well as in practice and expectations.

Another common view of education is that we need immediate results. We are an impatient nation and the payoff for teaching with understanding is often long-term. This requires articulation across levels as well as a change of expectations of what is learned and how it is learned. It depends upon a different view of accountability than we have now.

Teachers

I have saved to last what I consider the primary reason we have not made more progress. We often have failed to recognize the important contribution that teachers do and could make. Look at the history again. Colburn's description of what his book could do for teachers as well as Van Engen's and Wheat's acknowledgment of the teachers' role are quite different from what you will find in this book. Evident in this book is a position that respects and supports each teacher's knowledge, expertise, and beliefs. It is filled with the expectation that professionals, each with his or her own contributions, will work together as partners.

It is only when these views coincide that we will be able to make significant progress toward helping students develop understanding in mathematics. I believe that we are nearer to this confluence than in previous times, but the type of change called for in this book will not occur without involving the whole system and all the stakeholders of education. Just as changing one aspect of classroom practice will not suffice, changing only isolated classrooms will not be sufficient.

What Is This Book's Contribution to Developing Understanding?

In this book you will find guidance to begin or to renew your journey toward designing classrooms that encourage understanding. Each of us will find different ways to use this book as we think about understanding. Clearly, it influenced my thoughts about why we have not made more progress.

The view of understanding presented in Chapter 1 and illustrated throughout the book is deceptively simple. Actually it is broad and flexible, a definition that allows us to look at the many aspects of the proposed framework together and separately. The framework sets forth five dimensions: tasks, teacher's role, social culture, tools, and equity. The convergence of these dimensions along with the coherence of mathematical goals should help us move forward in building classrooms that provide all students the opportunity to build mathematical understandings that they can use throughout their lives.

Although I argued in the section about why we have not made progress that the developing of understanding cannot be done by adjusting only one dimension of your teaching, there are steps we can take to help us. Perhaps you will want to begin by looking at the nature of the mathematical tasks that you are presently using in your class. Do those tasks have the important characteristics of encouraging reflection and communication? Are there some ways that you can turn the tasks you are now using into ones that encourage understanding? What other aspects of mathematical tasks do you need to consider?

In this book you will find issues to discuss with colleagues to help you understand understanding. How does the social culture of your school affect the possibility of changing the culture of your classroom? Are there other mathematical tools needed in your classroom? How can you use mistakes as sites to encourage learning by everyone? How do you encourage students to share essential information? How do students determine the correctness of their mathematics? How do you involve each and every student in the sharing of their development of mathematical knowledge?

As you read and reflect on the examples of teaching, you will develop your own understanding of understanding. I found that one of the most meaningful paragraphs for me was in the story of Annie Keith's classroom. Describing that classroom (Chapter 7), the authors claim, "The constant is that students are always challenged to think and to try to make sense of what they are doing. They are challenged to take responsibility for monitoring their own learning and understanding. But learning is not an isolated individual activity; the students share ideas with one another and they learn from one another and learn to respect each other's ideas." As you read, find your own place where all the ideas seem to come together.

I firmly believe, as do the authors of this book, that the time for understanding has come and that it will become a part of our educational ethos. We have all learned from those that have espoused meaning or understanding in the past. This book adds to this discussion in a powerful way as it brings together many facets of the classroom—the tasks and tools, the teacher, the student, the environment, and the accessibility for and valuing of each and every student. It is a practical book that should help each and every one of us to reconsider what we are doing in our classrooms, whether they be at the grade levels described here, middle school, high school, college, or in our work with future and present teachers. No, you will not find all the answers for your own classroom, but you will find the important questions.

There are also positive signs that this is the time for understanding to be at the forefront because of the confluence of many of the forces that shape education. The information and changing world in which we live requires that we learn to learn, that we make the world understandable, and that we are confident of our abilities to do this. Mathematics in a technological world demands new skills and deeper understandings. The authors of this book use skill learning as a site for developing understanding, and build on the premise that this understanding allows for much deeper learnings.

The journey is not completed; we will continue to learn about teaching and learning with understanding. Along the way there will be milestones, one of which will be the ideas put forth in this book.

Mary Montgomery Lindquist

Columbus State University
Columbus, Georgia

Past-President
National Council of Teachers of Mathematics

Preface

This is a book about learning mathematics with understanding. What does it mean to design a classroom so that understanding is the primary goal? What would a system of instruction look like if we took seriously the goal of helping all students understand mathematics?

Our answers to these questions grew out of five years of discussions. Each of us are involved in ongoing projects that investigate the kinds of instruction that facilitate children's understanding of mathematics. At the invitation of the National Center for Research in Mathematical Sciences Education, we came together as a working group to examine the questions posed above. We shared our experiences and explored similarities and differences in the results of our projects and our interpretations of them. Although we shared the common goal of understanding what it means to teach for understanding, our individual projects are quite different and the similarities were not immediately apparent. Nevertheless, out of our continuing discussions grew a rather striking consensus about the features of classrooms that are essential for supporting students' understanding.

In this book we share our consensus about the essential features of classrooms for understanding mathematics. We also provide glimpses into our individual projects, and into the classrooms in which we have been spending time and from which we have drawn many of our ideas. By describing the essential features of classrooms that support students' mathematical understanding, and by providing pictures of several classrooms that exhibit these features, we hope to provide a framework within which teachers can reflect on their own practice, and think again about what it means to teach for understanding.

We wish to thank the many teachers and students who afforded us the opportunity of experiencing what it means to teach and learn mathematics with understanding. We also wish to thank the National Center for Research in Mathematical Sciences Education, University of

Wisconsin-Madison, and their granting agency, the Office of Educational Research and Improvement of the United States Department of Education (Grant No. R117G10002), for supporting our working group and making possible the preparation of this book. Of course, the opinions expressed in this book are ours and not necessarily those of the Office of Educational Research and Improvement.

1 *Introducing the Critical Features of Classrooms*

The world is changing. The societies that our students enter in the next decade and the next century will be different from those that we entered and different from those we see today. The workplace will be filled with new opportunities and new demands. Computers and new technologies are transforming the ways in which we do business, and future changes promise to be even more dramatic (Gates 1995). The skills needed for success will be different from those needed today. But the way in which societies will change, and the skills required of its citizens, are not fully predictable. Change is surely coming, but its exact nature is not entirely clear.

In order to take advantage of new opportunities and to meet the challenges of tomorrow, today's students need flexible approaches for defining and solving problems. They need problem-solving methods that can be adapted to new situations, and they need the know-how to develop new methods for new kinds of problems. Nowhere are such approaches more critical than in the mathematics classroom. Not only is technology making some conventional skills obsolete—such as high levels of speed and efficiency with paper-and-pencil calculations—it is also underscoring the importance of learning new and flexible ways of thinking mathematically.

All of this means that students must learn mathematics with understanding. Understanding is crucial because things learned with understanding can be used flexibly, adapted to new situations, and used to learn new things. Things learned with understanding are the most useful things to know in a changing and unpredictable world. There may be debate about what mathematical content is most important to teach. But there is growing consensus that whatever students learn, they should learn with understanding (National Council of Teachers of Mathematics [NCTM] 1989, 1991; Mathematical Sciences Education Board [MSEB] 1988).

1

Although important, usefulness is not the only reason to learn with understanding. If we want students to know what mathematics is, as a subject, they must understand it. Knowing mathematics, *really knowing it*, means understanding it. When we memorize rules for moving symbols around on paper we may be learning something, but we are not learning mathematics. When we memorize names and dates we are not learning history; when we memorize titles of books and authors we are not learning literature. Knowing a subject means getting inside it and seeing how things work, how things are related to each other, and why they work like they do.

Understanding is also important because it is one of the most intellectually satisfying experiences, and, on the other hand, not understanding is one of the most frustrating and ultimately defeating experiences. Students who are given opportunities to understand, from the beginning, and who work to develop understanding are likely to experience the kind of internal rewards that keep them engaged. Students who lack understanding and must resort to memorizing are likely to feel little sense of satisfaction and are likely to withdraw from learning. Many of us can recall instances from our own study of mathematics that resonate with these contrasting experiences. Understanding breeds confidence and engagement; not understanding leads to disillusionment and disengagement.

We begin, then, with the premise that understanding should be the most fundamental goal of mathematics instruction, the goal upon which all others depend. We believe that students' understanding is so important that it is worth rethinking how classrooms can be designed to support it. What kinds of classrooms facilitate mathematical understanding? That is the question this book is all about.

A Framework for Thinking About Classrooms

A primary thesis of this book is that classrooms that facilitate mathematical understanding share some core features, and that it is possible to tell whether classrooms support the development of understanding by looking for these features. In order to identify the features that support students' understanding, we need to set up a framework for analyzing classrooms. Our framework consists of five dimensions that work together to shape classrooms into particular kinds of learning environments: (a) the nature of the learning tasks, (b) the role of the teacher, (c) the social culture of the classroom, (d) the kind of mathematical tools that are available, and (e) the accessibility of mathematics for every student. We have found this framework useful because all classrooms can be analyzed along these five dimensions, regardless of the instructional approach. But more than that, the features that we believe are critical for facilitating understanding are found within these five dimensions. This means that the five dimensions form a framework both for examining whether a classroom is facilitating the development of understanding, and for guiding those who are trying to move their classrooms toward this goal. In other words, the framework can be used by teachers to reflect on their own practice, and to think about how their practice might change.

In this book we will look closely at each of these five dimensions. By presenting descriptions of each dimension and telling stories of classrooms that illustrate how the dimensions play out in real settings, we will identify what we think is essential for facilitating understanding and what is not. Some features within each dimension seem to be crucial for understanding, others seem to be optional. Through our explanations and illustrations, we will highlight the features that we believe are essential.

The book is organized into four parts. This introductory chapter provides an overview of what is to come. The chapter introduces many of the main ideas and raises questions that the reader might reflect on throughout the book. The second part consists of five brief chapters (Chapters 2–6) that describe the critical dimensions of classrooms designed for learning with understanding. Each chapter deals with one dimension and identifies and exemplifies those features that are essential for facilitating understanding. The third part illustrates how the critical features of classrooms can look in action. The four chapters (Chapters 7–10) each tell a story of a classroom. Although the classrooms may look different to a casual observer, we believe they share several core features within each dimension. The fourth part (Chapter 11) concludes the book by considering again the five dimensions, reviewing the critical features within each, and summarizing the ways in which these features can work together in classrooms.

Learning with Understanding

Most teachers would say that they want their students to understand mathematics, and in fact, that they teach for understanding. Teachers generally believe that understanding is a good thing. However, we have not always had a clear idea of what it means to learn mathematics with understanding, and we have had even less of an idea about how to tell whether a classroom was designed to facilitate understanding.

The reform efforts in mathematics education have, once again, directed the spotlight on understanding. Fortunately, we now are able to give a more complete description of what it means to learn with understanding and to teach for understanding. The reform documents themselves (NCTM 1989, 1991; MSEB 1988) provide some rich descriptions of what mathematical understanding looks like. The first four standards in NCTM's 1989 document highlight the importance of reasoning clearly, communicating effectively, drawing connections within mathematics and between mathematics and other fields, and solving real problems. All of these activities contribute to understanding and provide evidence for understanding.

Definition of Understanding

One of the reasons that it has been difficult to describe understanding in classrooms is that understanding is very complex. It is not something that you have or do not have. It is something that is always changing and growing. And understanding can be described from many different points of view. Because of its importance and complexity, there have been a number of recent descriptions of mathematical understanding, including those by Carpenter and Lehrer (1996), Davis (1992), Pirie and Kieren (1994), and Putnam et al. (1990). The reader may want to consult these and other sources for related but somewhat different descriptions of understanding.

[handwritten margin note: understanding connected, built over time]

A definition of understanding that works well for our purposes is one that has developed over many years and owes its existence to many psychologists and educators who have used and refined it in many contexts, including mathematics. This definition says that we understand something if we see how it is related or connected to other things we know (Brownell 1935; Hiebert and Carpenter 1992). For example, a teacher understands her student's anxiety about taking tests if she can relate the anxiety to other things she knows about the student, the current situation, and situations that the student may have encountered in the past. If she knows that the student has recently performed poorly on a major exam or that the student works very slowly and has trouble finishing tests on time, then she usually thinks she understands the student's anxiety a little better. The more relationships she can establish, the better she understands.

As another example, a student understands how to add 35 and 47 if she can relate this problem to other things she knows about addition and about the meaning of the numerals 35 and 47. Knowing that 35 is 3 tens and 5 ones and that 47 is 4 tens and 7 ones helps her understand several ways of combining the numbers. In both these cases, evidence for understanding is often provided in the form of explanations for why things are like they are, why the student is anxious, and why 35 and 47 is 82. Explanations are usually filled with connections, either implicit or explicit, between the target situation and other things that the person knows.

The definition of understanding in terms of relationships or connections works fine as a definition, but it does not reveal much about how people make connections. Furthermore, not all connections are equally useful. Some provide real insights and others are quite trivial. Some may even be inappropriate. To help think about how people make connections in mathematics and how they make connections that are useful, it is helpful to consider two processes that play an important role in the making of connections: reflection and communication.

Understanding Through Reflecting and Communicating

Two traditions in psychology have influenced our thinking about how students learn and understand mathematics—cognitive psychology with its emphasis on internal mental operations, and social cognition with its emphasis on the context of learning and social interaction (Hiebert 1992). The process of reflection is central for cognitive psychology, and the process of communication is central for social cognition. Although reflection and communication oversimplify these complex and influential traditions, they work well for our purposes because they provide important insights into how students construct understandings of mathematics and why the five dimensions of classrooms that we identified earlier are critical.

Reflection occurs when you consciously think about your experiences. It means turning ideas over in your head, thinking about things from different points of view, stepping back to look at things again, consciously thinking about what you are doing and why you are doing it. All of these activities have great potential for recognizing and building relationships between ideas or facts or procedures. In other words, stopping to think carefully about things, to reflect, is almost sure to result in establishing new relationships and checking old ones. It is almost sure to increase understanding.

Communication involves talking, listening, writing, demonstrating, watching, and so on. It means participating in social interaction, sharing thoughts with others and listening to others share their ideas. It is possible, of course, to communicate with oneself (reflection often involves such communication), but we will focus primarily on communication with others. By communicating we can think together about ideas and problems. This allows many people to contribute suggestions, so that we often can accomplish more than if we worked alone. Furthermore, communication allows us to challenge each other's ideas and ask for clarification and further explanation. This encourages us to think more deeply about our own ideas in order to describe them more clearly or to explain or justify them.

Communication works together with reflection to produce new relationships and connections. Students who reflect on what they do and communicate with others about it are in the best position to build useful connections in mathematics.

If it is true that reflection and communication foster the development of connections, then classrooms that facilitate understanding will be those in which students reflect on, and communicate about, mathematics. The question now becomes one of determining what kinds of classrooms encourage such activity. We believe that the five dimensions we identified earlier capture the aspects of classrooms that do just that. Before we explore these dimensions, we should deal with a common concern about understanding.

Is There a Trade-off Between Understanding and Skill?

Learning computational skills and developing conceptual understanding are frequently seen as competing objectives. If you emphasize understanding, then skills suffer. If you focus on developing skills, then understanding suffers. We believe that this analysis is wrong. It is not necessary to sacrifice skills for understanding, nor understanding for skills. In fact, they should develop together. In order to learn skills so they are remembered, can be applied when they are needed, and can be adjusted to solve new problems, they must be learned with understanding.

To some readers it may seem a bit ironic, but we have found that the learning of skills provides an ideal site for developing understanding. If students are asked to work out their own procedures for calculating answers to arithmetic problems and to share their procedures with others, they will necessarily be engaged in reflecting and communicating. Students who develop their own procedures for solving a problem, rather than imitating the procedure given in a textbook or demonstrated by the teacher, must reflect on the meaning of the numbers in the problem and on the operation involved in the calculation. Sharing their work involves more than just demonstrating a procedure; it requires describing, explaining, justifying, and so on as they are asked questions by their peers.

In spite of our belief that understanding and skills can and should develop together, we must make it clear that we assume the primary goal of mathematics instruction is conceptual understanding. But we must also make it clear that setting conceptual understanding as the primary goal does not mean ignoring computation skills. In fact, we have found that instruction for understanding can help students construct skills that can be recalled when needed, can be adjusted to fit new situations, and can be applied flexibly. In a word, we have found that such instruction can help students construct skills that they can actually use.

Dimensions and Core Features of Classrooms

Classroom instruction, of any kind, is a system. It is made up of many individual elements that work together to create an environment for learning. This means that instruction is much more than the sum total of all the individual elements. The elements interact with each other. It is difficult, if not impossible, to change one element in the system without altering the others. For example, suppose a teacher wanted to change the kinds of questions she asked. It is unlikely that she could change just the questions and leave everything else the same. Most likely, the nature of students' responses would change, the tasks for the students would change (at least the way students perceived the tasks), the ways in which the teacher listened and responded to students' responses would change, and so on. To repeat, instruction is a system, not a collection of individual elements, and the elements work together to create a particular kind of learning environment.

The dimensions we describe can be thought of as sets of features that are clustered around common themes. None of these dimensions, by itself, is responsible for creating a learning environment that facilitates students' constructions of understandings. Rather, they all work together to create such environments. Each of them is necessary, but not one, by itself, is sufficient.

The dimensions can also be thought of as a set of guidelines that teachers can use to move their instruction toward the goal of understanding. Just as students continually work toward richer understandings of mathematics, teachers continually work toward richer understandings of what it means to teach for understanding. The dimensions, and the core features within each dimension, provide guidelines and benchmarks that teachers can use as they reflect on their own practice.

The five dimensions will be described briefly here, and then elaborated in the following chapters. These introductions are intended to provide preliminary pictures of our classrooms. They herald the major issues that will appear throughout the book.

The Nature of Classroom Tasks

The nature of the tasks that students complete define for them the nature of the subject and contribute significantly to the nature of classroom life (Doyle 1983, 1988). The kinds of tasks that students are asked to perform set the foundation for the system of instruction that is created. Different kinds of tasks lead to different systems of instruction.

Features of
"Tasks"

We believe that a system of instruction which affords students opportunities to reflect and communicate is built on tasks that are genuine problems for students. These are tasks for which students have no memorized rules, nor for which they perceive there is one right solution method. Rather, the tasks are viewed as opportunities to explore mathematics and come up with reasonable methods for solution.

Appropriate tasks have at least three features (Hiebert et al. 1996). First, the tasks make the subject *problematic* for students. We do not use this term to mean that students do not understand mathematics or that it is frustrating for them. Rather, problematic means that students see the task as an interesting problem. They see that there is something to find out, something to make sense of. Second, the tasks must connect with where students are. Students must be able to use the knowledge and skills they already have to begin developing a method for completing the task. Third, the tasks must engage students in thinking about important mathematics. That is, they must offer students the opportunity to reflect on important mathematical ideas, and to take something of mathematical value with them from the experience.

The Role of the Teacher

The role of the teacher is shaped by the goal of facilitating conceptual understanding. This means that the teacher sets tasks that are genuine mathematical problems for students so that they can reflect on and communicate about mathematics. Instead of acting as the main source of mathematical information and the evaluator of correctness, the teacher now has the role of selecting and posing appropriate sequences of problems as opportunities for learning, sharing information when it is essential for tackling problems, and facilitating the establishment of a classroom culture in which pupils work on novel problems individually and interactively, and discuss and reflect on their answers and methods. The teacher relies on the reflective and conversational problem-solving activities of the students to drive their learning.

This role of the teacher differs dramatically from the more traditional role in which the teacher feels responsible to tell students the important mathematical information, demonstrate the procedures, and then ask students to practice what they have seen and heard until they become proficient. Such a role fits with a system of instruction in which understanding is believed to come by listening carefully to what the teacher says. It does not fit a system in which understanding is constructed by students through solving problems.

The role we describe for the teacher does not exclude the teacher from participating in class discussions and sharing information with the students. The teacher is actively engaged in helping the students construct understandings. However, by intervening too much and too deeply, the teacher can easily cut off students' initiative and creativity, and can remove the problematic nature of the material. The balance between allowing students to pursue their own ways of thinking and providing important information that supports the development of significant mathematics is not an easy one to achieve (Ball 1993b; Dewey 1933; Lampert 1991). Indeed, it constitutes a central issue in defining the appropriate role of the teacher, an issue that will be revisited later.

The Social Culture of the Classroom

A classroom is a community of learners. Communities are defined, in part, by how people relate to and interact with each other. Establishing a community in which students build understandings of mathematics means establishing certain expectations and norms for how students interact with each other about mathematics. It must be remembered that interacting is not optional: it is essential, because, as we noted earlier, communication is necessary for building understandings. So, the question is not whether students should interact about mathematics, but how they should interact.

What kind of social culture fits with the system of instruction we are describing? What features are needed to create a social culture that would support the kinds of tasks and reinforce the role of the teacher that we have described? These are important questions because whether tasks are authentic problems for students, problems that allow and encourage reflection and communication, depends as much on the culture of the classroom as on the tasks themselves (Hiebert et al. 1996).

We can identify four features of the social culture that encourage students to treat tasks as real mathematical problems. The first is that ideas are the currency of the classroom. Ideas, expressed by any participant, have the potential to contribute to everyone's learning and consequently warrant respect and response. Ideas deserve to be appreciated and examined. Examining an idea thoughtfully is the surest sign of respect, both for the idea and its author. A second core feature of the social culture is the autonomy of students with respect to the methods used to solve problems. Students must respect the need for everyone to understand their own methods, and must recognize that there are often a variety of methods that will do the job. The freedom to explore alternative methods and to share their thinking with their peers leads to a third feature: an appreciation for mistakes as learning sites. Mistakes must be seen by the students and the teacher as places that afford opportunities to examine errors in reasoning, and thereby raise everyone's level of analysis. Mistakes are not to be covered up; they are to be used constructively. A final core feature of the social culture of classrooms is the recognition that the authority for reasonability and correctness lies in the logic and structure of the subject, rather than in the social status of the participants. The persuasiveness of an explanation or the correctness of a solution depends on the mathematical sense it makes, not on the popularity of the presenter. Recognition of this is a key toward creating a constructive community of learners.

Mathematical Tools as Learning Supports

A common impression is that the reform movement in mathematics instruction is mostly a recommendation to use physical materials to teach mathematics. We believe that the reform movement is about much more than using physical materials. We also believe that the discussion of mathematical tools would benefit from broadening the definition to include oral language, written notation, and any other tools with which students can think about mathematics.

Mathematical tools should be seen as supports for learning. But using tools as supports does not happen automatically. Students must construct meaning for them. This requires more than watching demonstrations; it requires working with tools over extended periods of time, trying them out, and watching what happens. Meaning does not reside in tools; it is constructed by students as they use tools.

In mathematics classrooms, just as in everyday activities, tools should be used to accomplish something. In the classrooms we are describing, this means that tools should be used to solve problems. Mathematical tools can help solve problems by functioning in a variety of ways. They can provide a convenient record of something already achieved (e.g., using written symbols to record the partial results while solving a multistep problem); they can be used to communicate more effectively (e.g., using square tiles to explain a method for finding the area of a surface); and they can be used as an aid for thinking (e.g., using base-ten blocks to see how 321 can be decomposed before subtracting 87).

Regardless of the particular tools that are used, they are likely to shape the way we think. Mathematical activity requires the use of tools, and the tools we use influence the way we think about the activity. Another way to say this is that tools are an essential resource and support for building mathematical understanding, and the tools students use influence the *kinds* of understandings they develop (Fuson et al. 1992). Remember that understanding is a complicated thing. It is not all or nothing. It is made up of many connections or relationships. Some tools help students make certain connections; other tools encourage different connections.

An example can be drawn from second-grade arithmetic. When students are first learning to add and subtract numbers with two or more digits, there are many tools they might use. These include base-ten blocks, connecting cubes, hundreds charts, flip cards, written numbers, as well as language skills such as counting by tens and using a special vocabulary that highlights the tens and ones groupings (e.g., 18 is 1 ten and 8 ones). It is possible to imagine any of these tools being used in classrooms that incorporate the core features mentioned earlier: classrooms in which students encounter genuine problems; where the teacher encourages students to work out and share their own strategies; and where students respect each other's ideas. In other words, it is possible to imagine students using any of these tools to construct understandings. But it is also reasonable to believe that different tools may encourage different understandings. Students who use base-ten blocks may tend to develop different strategies (and consequently learn somewhat different things about numbers) than students who build on well-developed counting skills (this is a complex issue and will be examined further in Chapter 5). It should be noted that some of the variability apparent in the stories of classrooms (Chapters 7–10) is due to different choices of tools.

Equity and Accessibility

We believe that every student has the right to understand what they do in mathematics. Every student has the right to reflect on, and communicate about, mathematics. Understanding is not just the privilege of the high-achieving group. This is not a blue-sky belief that is out of touch with reality. Our experience is that, given classrooms like those we describe here, girls and boys at all levels of achievement and from all backgrounds can understand what they do in mathematics. More than that, understanding supports improved performance for students at all levels (Carey et al. 1993; Hiebert and Wearne 1993; Hiebert et al. 1991). That is, understanding is just as important for low achievers as for high achievers if we hope to raise levels of achievement above those in the past.

Equitable opportunities for all students sit squarely on the core features of classrooms described to this point. Tasks of the kind described in Chapter 2 must be accessible, at some level, to all students. The role of the teacher (Chapter 3) and the social culture of the classroom (Chapter 4) both point to the necessity of listening carefully to what each student says with a genuine interest in the ideas expressed (Paley 1986). Listening in this way does two things: It conveys a fundamental respect for the student, and it allows the teacher and peers to know the student as an individual. Both of these remove stereotypes and eliminate expectations that might be tied to particular group memberships. Equity, in part, means that each student is treated as an individual, and listening, *really listening*, is one of the best ways to encourage such treatment.

Equity contributes to the other dimensions as well as being a natural consequence of them. Establishing an appropriate social culture, for example, depends on every student participating as a member of the mathematics community. Learning opportunities arise as different ideas and points of view are expressed. To the extent that some students do not participate in the community, the learning opportunities are constrained. A rich, fully functioning community requires everyone's participation.

It is important to note that the notion of equity, as we interpret it, is not an add-on or an optional dimension. It is an integral part of a system of instruction that sets students' understanding of mathematics as the goal. Without equity, the other dimensions are restricted and the system does not function well. All five dimensions and the critical features within each are needed for the system to work.

Figure 1–1 provides a summary of the five dimensions and the features within each that we think are essential. Readers might wish to refer to the figure as a reminder of the major points in this chapter, and as an advance organizer for Chapters 2–6. These chapters will describe the core features in more detail and also will identify some optional features within the dimensions.

DIMENSIONS	CORE FEATURES
Nature of Classroom Tasks	Make mathematics problematic Connect with where students are Leave behind something of mathematical value
Role of the Teacher	Select tasks with goals in mind Share essential information Establish classroom culture
Social Culture of the Classroom	Ideas and methods are valued Students choose and share their methods Mistakes are learning sites for everyone Correctness resides in mathematical argument
Mathematical Tools as Learning Supports	Meaning for tools must be constructed by each user Used with purpose--to solve problems Used for recording, communicating, and thinking
Equity and Accessibility	Tasks are accessible to all students Every student is heard Every student contributes

1–1 Summary of dimensions and core features of classrooms that promote understanding

History of This Project

This book is an outgrowth of the collaboration of researchers from four research and development projects. During the past five years we met regularly to discuss our projects and examine differences and similarities in our approaches. Out of our discussions emerged a gradual but growing consensus about the essential features of classrooms that are designed to support students' understanding. This book describes our consensus. It represents our best collective thinking about these issues, thinking that is informed by evidence we have collected, observations of many different kinds of classrooms, discussions with many different teachers, and our reflections and communications with each other.

All of our projects focus on arithmetic in elementary school, with special attention to students' initial learning of multidigit addition and subtraction. This means that most of our examples will be taken from these topics and that the classroom stories presented later will describe lessons that involve whole number arithmetic. Although we recognize that other mathematics topics present some unique, specific questions, we believe that many of the issues we address and observations we provide are appropriate for mathematics teaching and learning in general. We pitched our descriptions at a level that could be applied to the teaching of any mathematical topic. For example, the five dimensions we identified and the core features within those dimensions are equally applicable to a range of topics and ages of students. Readers who would like to apply the ideas to, say, the teaching of percent in seventh grade, might need to build a few bridges on their own, but we believe that the crucial ideas are sufficiently alike that such constructions are possible.

The four projects were all conceived with an eye toward increasing students' understanding. Evidence of attention to the five dimensions of classrooms are apparent in each project, but with different configurations and different emphases. In order to provide a sense of the roots of our collective thinking, it is useful to provide a brief glimpse into the nature of the projects.

The four projects, in alphabetical order, are Cognitively Guided Instruction (CGI) directed by Thomas Carpenter, Elizabeth Fennema, and Megan Franke at the University of Wisconsin–Madison; Conceptually Based Instruction (CBI) directed by James Hiebert and Diana Wearne at the University of Delaware; Problem Centered Learning (PCL) directed by Piet Human, Hanlie Murray, and Alwyn Olivier at the University of Stellenbosch in South Africa; and Supporting Ten-Structured Thinking (STST) directed by Karen Fuson at Northwestern University.

All of the projects study learning and teaching in elementary classrooms, but they do so in somewhat different ways. CGI does not develop curricula nor design instruction. The primary goal is to help teachers acquire knowledge of children's mathematical thinking and then to study how teachers use their knowledge to design and implement instruction. CBI and STST design new instruction, work with teachers to implement it, and study the nature of students' learning in these classrooms. PCL is a large curriculum development and teacher training project. Teaching and learning are studied as teachers implement the PCL approach.

Despite the different orientations of the projects, the classrooms involved in each project show some striking similarities. The learning of basic number concepts and skills is viewed as a problem-solving activity rather than as the transmission of rules and procedures. Teachers allow students the time needed to develop their own procedures and do not expect all students to use the same ones. Class discussions involve sharing alternative methods and examining why they work. Teachers play an active role by posing problems, coordinating discussions, and joining students in asking questions and suggesting alternatives. In short, it appears that classrooms across the four projects employ the system of instruction we will describe, and exhibit the core features shown in Figure 1–1.

Differences also exist, not only among classrooms in different projects, but among classrooms within the same project. The differences arise from differences in the tasks selected, the kind of information provided, and the tools used to solve problems. For example, in some of the STST studies and in the CBI classrooms, students work with base-ten blocks and are helped to build connections between the blocks and written numerals, and between joining and separating actions on the blocks and adding and subtracting with numerals. In contrast, students in PCL classrooms do not use base-ten blocks and do not spend time building connections between structured manipulative materials and written numerals. Rather, they initially engage in a variety of counting activities and then develop arithmetic procedures from these understandings.

The contrast between these classrooms and the differences that would be immediately apparent to a casual observer highlight one of our central messages: Classrooms that promote understanding can look very different on the surface and still share the core features we have identified. Designing classrooms for understanding does not mean conforming to a single, highly prescribed method of teaching. Rather, it means taking ownership of a system of instruction, and then fleshing out its core features in a way that makes sense for a particular teacher in a particular setting. Chapters 7–10 illustrate further the ways in which classrooms can look different and still be very much the same.

Summary

Out of our four projects has emerged a consensus about what it means to understand mathematics and what is essential for facilitating students' understanding. We agree on the following principles: First, understanding can be characterized by the kinds of relationships or connections that have been constructed between ideas, facts, procedures, and so on. Second, there are two cognitive processes that are key in students' efforts to understand mathematics—reflection and communication. Third, there are five dimensions that play a prominent role in defining classrooms in terms of the kinds of learning that they afford: the nature of the tasks students are asked to complete, the role of the teacher, the social culture of the classroom, the mathematical tools that are available, and the extent to which all students can participate fully in the mathematics community of the classroom. Fourth, there are core features within these dimensions that afford students the opportunity to reflect on and communicate about mathematics, to construct mathematical understandings.

In the remainder of the book, we address these issues in more detail and provide extensive illustrations of how classrooms might look. Although we draw on our immediate experience working with primary-grade students on multidigit addition and subtraction and present many examples from this work, there are general principles here that could be applied to other age groups and other mathematical topics. We trust that we have shaped our descriptions and discussions so that such applications are possible for the reader to make.

2 *The Nature of Classroom Tasks*

One of the most important points that we will make is that students develop mathematical understanding as they invent and examine methods for solving mathematical problems. This is quite different than the usual claim which says that students acquire understanding as they listen to clear explanations by the teacher and watch the teacher demonstrate how to solve problems. In this chapter, we will explain what we mean when we say that students should be encouraged to invent and examine methods for solving problems, and we will show why this is essential for building important mathematical understandings.

Why Are Tasks Important?

Students learn from the kind of work they do during class, and the tasks they are asked to complete determines the kind of work they do (Doyle 1983, 1988). If they spend most of their time practicing paper-and-pencil skills on sets of worksheet exercises, they are likely to become faster at executing these skills. If they spend most of their time watching the teacher demonstrate methods for solving special kinds of problems, they are likely to become better at imitating these methods on similar problems. If they spend most of their time reflecting on the way things work, on how various ideas and procedures are the same or different, on how what they already know relates to the situations they encounter, they are likely to build new relationships. That is, they are likely to construct new understandings. How they spend their time is determined by the tasks that they are asked to complete. The tasks make all the difference.

Students also form their perceptions of what a subject is all about from the kinds of tasks they do. If they are asked in history class only to memorize the names, dates, and locations of historical events, they will think that history is about remembering facts from the past. If students are asked in mathematics class only to practice prescribed procedures by completing sets of exercises, they will think that mathematics is about following directions to move symbols around as quickly as possible. If we want students to think that doing mathematics means solving problems, they will need to spend most of their time solving problems. Students' perceptions of the subject are built from the kind of work they do, not from the exhortations of the teacher. These perceptions guide their expectations for what they will do in mathematics class and influence their inclination to participate in the kind of classroom community we are describing in this book (see Chapter 4). Once again, it starts with the tasks. The tasks are critical.

What Kinds of Tasks Are Important?

What kinds of tasks should teachers use if they want their students to build important mathematical understandings? As we argued in Chapter 1, students build mathematical understandings by reflecting and communicating, so the tasks must allow and encourage these processes. This requires several things: First, the tasks must allow the students to treat the situations as problematic, as something they need to think about rather than as a prescription they need to follow. Second, what is problematic about the task should be the mathematics rather than other aspects of the situation. Finally, in order for students to work seriously on the task, it must offer students the chance to use skills and knowledge they already possess. Tasks that fit these criteria are tasks that can leave behind something of mathematical value for students. We will explore these criteria for selecting and designing tasks in the next section.

Characteristics of Tasks

Tasks Should Encourage Reflection and Communication

Reflecting and communicating are the processes through which understanding develops. One of the simplest principles we can suggest is that if you would like students to understand, then be sure they are reflecting on what they are doing and communicating about it to others. Tasks are the key. They provide the context in which students can reflect on and communicate about mathematics.

Reflecting means turning something over in your head, thinking again about it, trying to relate it to something else you know. If a task encourages you to reflect on something, you do not rush through it as quickly as you can. Tasks that encourage reflection take time. Communicating means talking and listening. It means sharing the method you developed to solve a problem and responding to questions about your method. It means listening to others share their methods and asking questions to make sure you understand.

In order for students to reflect on mathematics and communicate their experience, they must see that there is something intriguing on which to reflect and something worthwhile to communicate. They must sense a difficulty that they would like to resolve and discuss. In order for the task to meet these needs, two things are essential: one is that students must make the task their own. Students must set the goal of solving the problem. The second is that the intriguing or perplexing part of the situation should be the *mathematics*. The task could, of course, be interesting in lots of ways, but if students are to build *mathematical* understandings, then it should be interesting in a mathematical way.

Ownership

For something to be a problem for a student, he or she must see it as a challenge and must want to know the answer. The student must set a goal of resolving the problem. The goal might come from the student, or be adopted by the student after listening to peers or the teacher. The important thing is that the student makes the goal his or her own.

Goals come in many shapes and sizes: A goal might be to find the answer to a question posed by the teacher or by peers; it might be to increase the efficiency of a computation procedure; it might be to develop a strategy to solve a large, messy problem; it might be to generate a problem for others to solve. All of these goals define problems for students. They set intellectual challenges that create the need for resolution. The goals might set short-term problems, solvable in a few minutes, or they might set long-term, large-scale problems, solvable only after days or weeks.

Students will work to achieve goals only if they believe the goals are worth the effort. The reasons for perceiving worth may include the student's personal values (remember that all students are naturally curious) or values emerging in the culture of the classroom (for example, students may wish to participate in the class discussion and have something to contribute; see Chapters 3 and 4). It is important that the student attaches worth to the goal beyond that of immediate external rewards (Hatano 1988). If students are working only toward an external reward, such as leaving for recess early, this can work against reflecting thoughtfully about what they are doing.

Some tasks suggest interesting problematic situations that are not very mathematical. For example, suppose a group of sixth graders was given a budget of $100 and asked to plan a class party. This kind of task has become a favorite mathematical activity. However, the task may be resolved with little mathematics, especially of a kind that would challenge sixth graders. The situation still might be problematic, but the problems raised and resolved might be social or political ones.

The reverse can also occur. Some situations might look mathematical but would not be very problematic. For example, suppose a student, say Joanne, wanted to memorize the multiplication facts, perhaps to please her parents, or her teacher, or even herself. She borrowed a set of flash cards from her teacher and drilled herself for a number of days until she knew them all. Although we might applaud Joanne's motivation and discipline, and agree that knowing multiplication facts is important, we would not say that she engaged in solving a problem. The activity might even be called mathematical, but it did not make mathematics problematic. There was no need to search for and develop a method to solve the problem, and there was no need to reflect on what was happening. This is important because it means that it is unlikely that the activity facilitated the development of Joanne's mathematical understanding. We are not saying the activity was wasteful or unimportant: The point is that understanding develops only as students reflect on and communicate about situations that are mathematically problematic.

Here is an example of a task that is mathematically problematic: Suppose students are presented with the task of developing a method for adding $\frac{1}{3} + \frac{1}{4}$. If students have not yet added fractions with unlike denominators, this could be a task that allows the mathematics to become problematic for students. They would need to rely on their past experiences and then extend their knowledge to generate a solution. They would need to reflect on what they know about fractions, perhaps use resources such as diagrams or fraction pieces, and continually think about whether the methods they are developing are consistent with methods for related problems and whether the answer that is produced is reasonable. All of this involves intensive reflection. If students are asked to work on the task in small groups or to present and defend their method of solution, then communication becomes an integral part of the activity. Communication increases the likelihood that students will think again about their own method, and hear about other methods that would work just as well or better. It is not hard to see that understanding would be a natural outcome of this kind of task.

Tasks Should Allow Students to Use Tools

Tasks that encourage reflection and communication are tasks that link up with students' thinking. One way to describe this is to say that students should see ways in which they can use the tools they possess to begin the task. We define tools broadly to include things the student already knows and materials that can be used to solve problems. Tools are resources or *learning supports*, as we will call them in Chapter 5, and include skills that have been acquired (e.g., counting and adding single-digit numbers can be used as tools to add multidigit numbers), physical materials (e.g., fraction pieces can be used to add $\frac{1}{3} + \frac{1}{4}$), written symbols (often used as records for things that have been figured out), and verbal language (often used to communicate with others about the task). We will describe the role of tools more completely in Chapter 5, so we will make only a few points here, in relation to tasks.

Using tools to work on mathematical tasks can be thought of like using tools to complete tasks around the home. Tools are very handy, and we use many of them without even thinking. We use our reading skill to study the directions for how to open the new aspirin bottle; we use water, detergent, and a dish cloth to wash the dishes; and we use our fingers to flip the latch on the window. How did we learn to use these tools so well? We learned to use them because we were given time to explore the tools and time to practice using them in different ways. Of course, it is likely that we also had a bit of instruction in how to use them, but we did not learn by sitting back and watching someone else use them. One does not learn to use a hammer skillfully by watching someone else hammer nails. Tools are used effectively when their owners can practice using them on a variety of tasks. It is the same way with mathematical tools. Students need to have time to explore them, try them out, and use them in a variety of situations.

A second thing about tools is that they are used when there is a need to use them, when they can help to solve a problem or complete a task. Tools are used for a purpose. It is likely that you did not practice using a dish cloth just so you could get good at it. There were dirty dishes that needed to be washed. The same is true for mathematical tools. Students get good at using mathematical tools by using them to solve problems. Usually there is little point in practicing with tools just to be practicing.

It is important to note that tools are used when the *user* sees a need for using them. This means two things: One is that the user chooses the tool to use and finds out if it was a good choice by using it. Choosing a sledge hammer rather than a nail hammer to pound in the tomato stake may not be the best choice (the sledge hammer may be too heavy for the thin stake) but the user will learn about sledge hammers and nail hammers and tomato stakes by trying it out. Something similar is true for mathematical tools. Counting by ones may not be the best tool to find 45 + 38, but the tool user will find out something valuable about counting by ones and about 45 + 38 by trying it out, reflecting on the process, and communicating with others about it.

Another implication of using tools when the user sees a need is that the tasks need to be suitable for the tools that are available. It would be inappropriate to ask someone to build an intricate piece of furniture if they had never used a saw or chisel. Building a wood crate for storing toys might be a better first task. Similarly, it would be inappropriate to ask students to solve $\frac{1}{4} + \frac{1}{3}$ if they did not yet know the meaning of $\frac{1}{4}$ and $\frac{1}{3}$. This does not mean that tasks should be easy for students, or that students should know how to complete them before they start. Rather, it means that students should already have some tools available that allow them to begin thinking about the problem and trying out methods that might work. After students have talked about fractions such as $\frac{1}{4}$ and $\frac{1}{3}$, and perhaps represented them with fraction pieces, then they have some tools they can use to begin solving $\frac{1}{4} + \frac{1}{3}$. Tasks should be challenges for students, but they should link up with where students are and with what they already know and can do.

Tasks Should Leave Behind Important Residue

William Brownell (1946) pointed out a number of years ago that it is better to think of understanding as that which comes naturally while students solve mathematical problems rather than as something we should teach directly. More recently, Davis (1992) suggested that we have too long been designing our curriculum and instruction on the idea that we should first teach students skills and then have students apply them to solve problems. Davis argued that it is better to *begin* with problems, allow students to develop methods for solving them, and recognize that what students take away from this experience is what they have learned. Such learning is likely to be deep and lasting. Davis referred to the learning that students take with them from solving problems as "residue."

The point that both Brownell and Davis were making is that we build understandings or relationships by discovering them and hearing about them and using them as we solve problems. Teachers can point out relationships, but they become meaningful as students use them for solving problems. For example, teachers can point out that 38 means 38 ones, or 3 tens and 8 ones, or 2 tens and 18 ones, and so on. But these relationships only become meaningful for students when they use them to solve problems. For example, if students solve 45 + 38 by adding 3 tens and 4 tens to get 70, and 8 ones and 5 ones to get 13 ones, and then combine these to get 83, then the relationships between tens and ones become significant.

Thinking of understandings as outcomes of solving problems rather than as concepts that we teach directly requires a fundamental change in our perceptions of teaching. Many of us have been brought up to think that the best way to teach mathematics is to teach important concepts, like place value or common denominators, by explaining them clearly and demonstrating how to use them and then having students practice them. Our recommendation is that we change our way of thinking and teaching so that students are allowed to develop concepts, such as place value and common denominators, in the context of solving problems. This means that when selecting tasks or problems, we need to think ahead about the kinds of relationships that students might take with them from the experience.

We cannot provide a list of all the residues that are important because there is no one correct list, and if there were it would be very long. There are many kinds of understandings that are important, and different students are likely to build different ones. We can, however, identify two types of residue that are essential and that can provide useful guides for selecting tasks. One type can be called insights into the structure of mathematics, and the second type is the strategies or methods for solving problems.

Mathematical systems are filled with relationships. Take the base-ten number system for an example. The simple looking numeral 328 is loaded with relationships that can be constructed by students—relationships between the values of the digits, between the units represented by the different positions, and so on. Tasks that invite students to explore relationships of this kind, while they are solving problems, are likely to leave behind insights into the structure of this mathematical system (Cobb et al. 1991; Fuson and Briars 1990; Hiebert and Wearne 1993).

Tasks that are likely to focus students' attention on mathematical relationships are tasks such as: developing several different methods for solving 28×17 and discussing the efficiency of the methods; finding how many triangles can be drawn inside a rectangle, pentagon, hexagon, and so on, using the vertices of the polygon, and looking for a pattern; and deciding whether it is possible to find a fraction between any two fractions and explaining why or why not. Tasks like this provide opportunities for students to get inside mathematical systems and discover how they work. In general, tasks that encourage students to reflect on mathematical relationships are likely to leave behind insights into structure.

If tasks are problematic for students, and if students are allowed to work out methods to complete the tasks, then they also are likely to take with them strategies for solving problems. Two kinds of strategies will be left as residue. One kind of strategy is a specific technique for completing specific kinds of tasks. Two quite different examples will help to illustrate this process. First, consider a routine-looking computation problem. Suppose students had not yet added decimal fractions and the task involved adding $1.34 + 2.5$. After students developed methods for completing the task they would likely take with them specific strategies that could be used to add similar decimal fractions in the future.

A second example comes from a larger scale real-life situation. The day we were writing the first draft of this chapter, Cal Ripken Jr. broke Lou Gehrig's record for consecutive games played in Major League baseball. Mr. Gehrig's record was 2130; Mr. Ripken was playing in his 2131st consecutive game. The Baltimore Orioles had especially large crowds during the weeks leading up to this event. On this day, they set up 260 extra seats for the game and charged $5000 for each seat, with the proceeds used to help find treatments and a cure for Lou Gehrig's disease. There are many questions that could be asked about this situation, including statistical comparisons of Mr. Gehrig's and Mr. Ripken's baseball careers, estimates on the number of people that have seen, in person, each of them play, and percentage of revenue from today's game that was contributed to fight Lou Gehrig's disease. Of course, to answer the questions students would need to do some additional research. Tasks like this provide experiences in finding, organizing, and manipulating lots of information. Students are likely to take with them a variety of specific techniques for organizing and manipulating numbers.

But it is likely that students will take with them another kind of strategy from solving both kinds of problems that is even more important than the specific techniques they acquire. As students develop their own methods for solving problems, they develop general approaches for inventing specific procedures or adapting ones they already know to fit new problems. In other words, they learn how to construct their own methods (Fennema et al. 1993; Hiebert and Wearne 1993; Kamii and Joseph 1989; Wearne and Hiebert 1989).

This kind of residue is extremely valuable because it enables students to solve a variety of problems without having to memorize different procedures for each new problem. Although students can acquire specific strategies for specific tasks through more traditional forms of instruction, we believe that they acquire general approaches for developing their own procedures only if they are allowed to treat tasks as problematic. In other words, students learn how to construct methods to solve problems if they are allowed to do just that.

A major advantage of thinking about learning as the residue that gets left behind when solving problems is that it provides a way of dealing with a very common difficulty. Many students have trouble connecting the concepts they are learning with the procedures they are practicing (Hiebert 1986). They often end up memorizing and practicing procedures that they do not understand (e.g., adding fractions with unlike denominators). This has damaging consequences, such as forgetting procedures, learning slightly flawed procedures without knowing it, or applying them rigidly without adjusting them for slightly different problems (National Assessment of Educational Progress 1983). In general, if students separate their conceptual understandings from their procedures it means that they cannot solve problems very well.

We believe that the reason so many students separate concepts and procedures, and acquire many procedures they do not understand, is that traditional instruction encourages this separation. By trying to teach concepts and procedures directly, we artificially separate them. Although we may try to get students to hook them back together, this is more difficult than we think and most students are not successful. They learn procedures by imitating and practicing rather than by understanding them, and it is hard to go back and try to understand a procedure after you have practiced it many times (Hatano 1988; Resnick and Omanson 1986; Wearne and Hiebert 1988a). Without understanding, it is easy to forget procedures and distort them. And it is hard to adjust them to solve different kinds of problems.

An alternative is to begin with problems. If students are encouraged to develop their own procedures for solving problems, then they must use what they already know, including the understandings they have already constructed. There is no other way to do it. Understandings and procedures remain tightly connected because procedures are built on understandings. The methods students first develop may not be the most efficient ones, but they will be methods students understand. This is exactly what we are finding in classrooms that treat arithmetic in this way (Carpenter et al. 1989; Hiebert and Wearne 1992, 1993, in press; Kamii and Joseph 1989; Murray et al. 1992).

We believe that if we want students to understand mathematics, it is more helpful to think of understanding as something that results from solving problems, rather than something we can teach directly. In particular, we believe that teaching concepts and procedures separately is potentially damaging. It is more appropriate to engage students in solving problems because it is only through solving problems that their concepts and procedures develop together and remain connected in a natural and productive way.

What Changes Should We Make in Our Current Curriculum?

In this chapter we have described the kinds of tasks that fit into the system of instruction we outlined in Chapter 1. Most of our discussion says more about *how* the content should be treated than *what* content should be included. The system of instruction that we recommend is an approach to treating content, not a prescription for the selection of content.

Nevertheless, we can say a few things about content: First, we believe that much of the content in current curricula, as presented in popular textbooks, is appropriate *as long as* students are allowed to make the mathematics problematic. The system of instruction we describe does not mean a wholesale replacement of the curriculum. In fact, there may be few content changes that are required.

A second point is that the reason for including particular topics may be different now than in the past. Arithmetic computation, for example, has occupied the lion's share of the curriculum in elementary school because of the importance that has been attached to rapid paper-and-pencil calculation skills. This is being challenged by the reform documents which point out that these skills are rapidly declining in importance (NCTM 1989). We agree that students do not need to become high-speed paper-and-pencil calculators; electronic calculators do that job better. The great amount of time spent practicing fast execution of paper-and-pencil procedures is better spent elsewhere. But we believe that computation is still an important topic (Hiebert 1990). It provides a rich site for students to develop methods for solving problems and to gain important understandings about the number systems and about operations within number systems. Studying computation serves as a vehicle for building mathematical understandings. Of course, it still is useful to possess some computation skills, but these develop alongside the insights into how numbers work as students develop their own methods and examine them carefully (Carpenter et al. 1989; Fennema et al. 1996; Hiebert and Wearne 1992, 1993, in press).

A third point about content is that the criteria identified earlier can be used to decide whether classroom tasks contain appropriate content. The task should allow and encourage students to problematize the mathematics of the situation, and it should invite students to use the tools they already possess to solve the problem. Such tasks are likely to leave behind something of mathematical value. These criteria cannot be used to select topics or to say that one topic is more important than another. But they do say that tasks should be selected for the mathematics of the situation, rather than other extraneous features and that, as one completes the task and looks back, the mathematics of the situation should be the most salient residue. Mathematics should be the focal point, both going into the task and coming out of the task.

Using these three criteria, it is easy to see that much of the content in the current curricula could be framed into tasks that would be appropriate. On the other hand, some tasks that are being proposed as innovative and reform-minded would be inappropriate. Simple computation problems, such as $38 + 45$ and $\frac{1}{4} + \frac{1}{3}$ can be mathematically problematic for students if they are introduced at the right time and treated appropriately, and they can leave behind important residue. In contrast, planning parties with $100 budgets might look interesting and engaging, but might have few mathematical goals going in and leave little mathematical residue coming out. When deciding whether a task is appropriate, it is helpful to look at the way in the which the goals students set will shape the task and the kind of mathematical understandings that are likely to be left behind.

Tasks Form the Foundation for Instruction

The system of instruction we outlined in Chapter 1 is an interrelated ensemble of five dimensions. Instruction depends on all five working together, and the nature of the tasks is only one of the five. Still, the tasks provide a foundation for instruction that is critical. The underlying processes of reflection and communication are possible only when the tasks are appropriately problematic. The entire system of instruction we are describing depends on tasks that allow and encourage students to treat mathematics as problematic. The way in which the other classroom dimensions build on these kinds of tasks will become clear in the next several chapters.

3 *The Role of the Teacher*

All teachers believe they have certain responsibilities in a mathematics class. For many teachers, these include explaining ideas clearly, demonstrating procedures so students can follow them, and encouraging plenty of practice so students can execute these procedures quickly and accurately. One of the major differences in the system of instruction we are describing is a change from these traditional responsibilities. The most important role for the teacher becomes creating a classroom in which all students can reflect on mathematics and communicate their thoughts and actions. Clear explanations and demonstrations from the teacher become less important than explanations and demonstrations by students. This is a different way to think about teaching. The roles and responsibilities change in very significant ways.

To describe the changes in the role of the teacher, we will focus on two responsibilities: providing direction for the mathematical activities of the class, and guiding the development of the classroom culture. We will spend most of the time with the first of these because the second is discussed more thoroughly in Chapter 4.

Providing Direction for Mathematical Activities

The Dilemma

We begin our discussion with the biggest problem for teachers: how to assist students in experiencing and acquiring mathematically powerful ideas but refrain from assisting so much that students abandon their own sense-making skills in favor of following the teacher's directions (Ball 1993b; Lampert 1991; Wheat 1941). To put it another way, how do teachers handle the tension between supporting the initiative and problem-solving abilities of students and, at the same time, promoting the construction of mathematically important concepts and skills? Or, using Ball's words, how do teachers develop "a practice that respects the integrity both of mathematics as a discipline *and* of children as mathematical thinkers" (376)?

In most school settings the tendency of students to rely on their own problem-solving abilities is very fragile. If they sense that the teacher expects them to solve problems in a certain way, they will abandon their own efforts to understand and will search for ways to satisfy the teacher. So teachers need to allow and promote students' autonomy (Kamii 1985; Kamii and Joseph 1989). They need to respect students as intellectual participants. On the other hand, if left on their own, students can spend a great deal of time floundering and making little progress. More than that, if teachers do not intervene at all, students are likely to miss a good deal of mathematics. The hands-off approach is overly conservative. It underestimates students' ability to make sense of powerful ideas and ways of thinking that teachers can share with them. In addition to respecting students as thinkers, teachers must respect mathematics as a discipline.

Can teachers resolve this dilemma? Not by following a rule or a recipe. In fact, Lampert (1985) argued that dilemmas like this one are a natural part of teaching. Rather than resolving the dilemma by choosing one of the options, and rather than resisting or ignoring the dilemma, teachers should embrace it. By remaining open to the tension, teachers can remain sensitive to both the subject and the students.

We agree with Lampert that this dilemma, and others, are not entirely resolvable. We also believe that there are productive ways in which teachers can deal with this dilemma. That is, we believe it is possible for teachers to intervene in ways that stimulate and push students' thinking forward and, at the same time, promote students' autonomy. The principle that guides decisions about how to achieve this balance is familiar by now: to create an environment in which students reflect on and communicate about mathematics. But we can be more specific.

Selecting and Designing Tasks

One of the most critical responsibilities for a teacher is setting appropriate tasks. As we noted earlier, appropriate tasks enable students to reflect on and communicate about mathematics. Although it is possible for students to share in selecting tasks, and teachers should always be aware of and open to students' participation, students are unlikely to select and invent tasks that, over time, will engage them in the full range of mathematical ideas. Teachers must assume responsibility for setting tasks.

Selecting Tasks with Goals in Mind

Our discussion of tasks has focused on the characteristics of individual tasks. These characteristics are useful for teachers as they decide whether particular tasks are appropriate. But the teacher's role in selecting tasks goes well beyond choosing good individual tasks, one after another. Teachers need to select sequences of tasks so that, over time, students' experiences add up to something important. Teachers need to consider the residue left by working on *sets* of tasks, not just individual tasks.

Students' understanding is built up gradually, over time, and through a variety of experiences. Understanding usually does not appear full-blown, after one experience or after completing one task. This means that the selection of appropriate tasks includes thinking about how tasks are related, how they can be chained together to increase the opportunities for students to gradually construct their understandings.

Tasks are related if they allow students to see the same idea from different points of view, or if they allow students to build later solution methods on earlier ones. Tasks that are related in these ways increase the coherence of students' mathematical experiences. By coherence we mean that, through the student's eyes, the sequence of activities and experiences fit together and make sense. Students see that they are not just engaged in a series of individual, random problem-solving activities, but that the activities are connected and are leading somewhere. There is good reason to believe that students take away deeper mathematical understandings when the mathematical activities are coherent, both within lessons and between lessons (Hiebert and Wearne 1992; Stigler and Perry 1988). And the way in which tasks are connected helps to establish this coherence.

How do teachers select tasks that, over time, help students weave together their individual experiences into a coherent whole? We believe that the selection of sequences of tasks must be guided by the teacher's vision of what the students can take with them over the course of the year and how these residues might be formed. Task sequences are selected that are consistent with the teacher's goals for students and the teacher's vision for how the goals might be achieved.

A third-grade class was just beginning to study multiplication. The teacher, Ms. Higachi, believed there were two kinds of residue that were important. She wanted the students to take away the notion that multiplication, as an operation, can be used to solve several different kinds of problems, and she wanted them to acquire a method for multiplying that they understood. Her vision also included the hypothesis that many students would connect multiplication initially to repeated addition and, although this connection would give them an initial method for solving the problems, she wanted them to see multiplication as more than repeated addition. Ms. Higachi used her vision to select a sequence of tasks through which students might, over time, form these residues. She used some of the tasks from the commercial textbook series and designed some of the tasks herself.

The first tasks selected by Ms. Higachi were story situations that described multiple groups of items. In some cases, the groups had different numbers of items and in some cases all the groups had the same number of items, say 7 boxes of doughnuts with 6 doughnuts in each box. Class discussions centered around comparing the different situations: noticing the differences in methods that could be used to find the total number of items, the kinds of units that were suggested in each situation (e.g., boxes and doughnuts), and differences in the ways the situations could be represented with written words and symbols. All of these differences pointed to something special about the situations which had the same number of items in each group. Ms. Higachi then introduced the multiplication symbol, $\times$, as a way of representing these special situations (e.g., $7 \times 6 = 42$, for 7 boxes of 6 doughnuts each is 42 doughnuts).

To begin their study of multiplication, Ms. Higachi had selected tasks that, together, would focus attention on the special features of the simplest multiplicative situations. These simple grouping situations also allowed students to develop solution methods that connected with their counting and addition skills. Although these kinds of tasks can be dealt with meaningfully by second graders, and even first graders, Ms. Higachi found, through conversations with her students, that most of them had not yet encountered these kinds of tasks, and so she decided to begin here.

In order to provide opportunities for students to enrich their understandings of multiplication, Ms. Higachi then presented a series of tasks that required a different way of thinking about multiplication. These tasks asked questions like the following: If you have 3 different kinds of meat, and 2 different kinds of cheese, how many different sandwiches can you make, putting 1 kind of meat and 1 kind of cheese in each sandwich? Over time, as students worked through a number of similar tasks, with materials available to act out the situations, the class discussions focused on the kinds of units in each situation, the methods that were used to find the solutions, and the ways the situations could be represented with written words and symbols. Ms. Higachi asked about similarities and differences between the first kinds of tasks and these tasks. Several students suggested that both types of problems could be solved using the same method (counting up by 6s, or 2s, etc.) even though the problems looked different at first. Ms. Higachi underscored this suggestion. She had, in fact, selected the sequence of tasks with this kind of residue in mind.

Over the course of the year, Ms. Higachi selected tasks representing other models of multiplication. One set of tasks included measuring the heights of plant seedlings that the students were growing and calculating the final height if the plants would eventually grow eight times as tall. Another set of tasks involved finding the area, in square units, of various rectangles. Discussions always focused on the units in the situation, the methods used to find the solutions, and the ways in which the situations could be represented with written words, numbers, and symbols.

Ms. Higachi knew that students would only begin building a full understanding of multiplication through interacting with these tasks. In later years, students would encounter a greater variety of multiplicative situations and would develop more efficient methods. Her goal for this year was to allow students to construct at least one solution method that they understood, and to develop the sense that multiplication encompasses a variety of problem situations.

We need to point out that Ms. Higachi's selection of tasks is only one possible sequence. There are other appropriate selections that could be made. We recounted Ms. Higachi's choice only to provide an illustration of how one teacher's vision of the residues that might be left from working with multiplication guided her selection of tasks. She believed these residues would be formed over time by working through a series of related problems, not by solving one (even very clever) problem. She understood how the problems students worked on in third grade might connect with those encountered before third grade and after third grade. Her vision guided the selection of the individual problems and how they were sequenced. Stories of other teachers selecting tasks with goals in mind are found in chapters 7–10 and other useful sources, such as Parker (1993).

Before leaving this section, we want to point out that there is another way of talking about this issue, a way that returns us to the dilemma for teachers. In this context, the dilemma becomes one of how to set goals and plan for instruction, over time, without removing students from the equation. In traditional systems of instruction, teachers often describe their mathematical goals by listing the skills and concepts they plan to teach. These goals then push teachers toward activities like demonstrating, explaining, showing, and so on because these are thought to be the best and clearest ways of teaching the skills and concepts. The trouble is that these plans often are based on objectives of covering material and do not consider carefully the kinds of residues that might get left behind. The plans often are not sensitive to what we know about how students construct understanding, and do not allow for the kind of reflection and communication that is essential.

In contrast, there is growing interest in nontraditional curricula that are filled with interesting problems, often large-scale real-life tasks. Teachers are to present the problems to students and allow them to work. Sometimes the work on a task will extend over a period of days or even weeks. The goals include engaging students in doing mathematics and solving the problems. The goals are not lists of skills and concepts. Although such programs place a positive emphasis on respecting students' autonomy and respecting their intellectual capabilities, the content goals often are unspecified. It can be difficult for teachers to identify the mathematical goals that can and should be planned for and worked toward during the year.

The system of instruction we are recommending takes a different approach than either of these two. As in the nontraditional approach, mathematics begins with problems. But, the system encourages teachers to use their learning goals for students, and their vision of how these goals might be achieved over time to select sequences of problems. Simon (1995) describes this vision as a "hypothetical learning trajectory." The trajectory is the teacher's vision of the mathematical path that the class might take, and its hypothetical nature comes from the fact that it is based on the teacher's guess about how learning might proceed along the path. The trajectory guides the teacher's task selection, but feedback from students and the teacher's assessments of the residues that are being formed lead to revisions in the trajectory. Tasks are selected purposefully, but the sequence can be revised.

Selecting coherent sets of tasks provides a way for teachers to enact or materialize their vision for what students can learn over the course of the year. Setting goals in terms of students' experiences and residues that might be left is a different way of thinking than the more traditional conceptions of goals as lists of instructional objectives. We believe it has the advantage of bringing together two notions that sometimes compete. Mathematics for students can begin with problems and, at the same time, teachers can set quite specific goals to guide the selection of tasks and, in turn, the mathematical activities of students. This provides one way of dealing with the dilemma described earlier.

Knowledge Needed to Select Tasks

What do teachers need to know to select or make up appropriate individual tasks and coherent sequences of tasks? The simple answer is that they need to have a good grasp of the important mathematical ideas and they need to be familiar with their students' thinking.

Grasping the important ideas means knowing the lay of the land. It means being familiar with the main markers and how they are arranged and how they can be rearranged. For example, in many fourth-grade classrooms, students are finishing their work on addition and subtraction of whole numbers, working seriously on multiplication and division of whole numbers, beginning work with fractions, measuring with standard units, and examining two-dimensional and three-dimensional figures. Selecting appropriate tasks for fourth graders requires knowing these topics—how they relate to each other and how they relate to more elementary (prior grades) and more advanced (succeeding grades) treatments of them. Teachers need to feel as if they can walk around in this terrain, getting from one location to another via a variety of routes (Greeno 1991). Such knowledge will help them construct sequences of tasks that spotlight the important mathematics, allow it to be problematic, and follow a path that moves sensibly through the terrain. The residue that is left from working on the tasks is likely to be relationships that help students to begin to find *their* way around in this terrain.

Teachers also need to know how their own students think about mathematical problems and how most students of similar age and experience are likely to solve problems. This information is crucial for two reasons: One is that it allows teachers to select tasks that link up with tools that students are likely to bring with them. The second is that it provides a clue about the kind of residue that might get left behind. In other words, information on students' thinking indicates how students might enter the situation and how they might leave. Obviously, this is valuable for selecting tasks that connect with where students are and that pull them in appropriate directions.

We have not always understood the importance of knowing how students think. Many classroom teachers, of course, have discovered that they can make better instructional decisions when they have this information. But, in general, we have not fully appreciated how critical and how helpful such information is for planning instruction. Recently, a good deal of research has been conducted as part of the Cognitively Guided Instruction project (see Chapters 1 and 7) that has demonstrated the good use teachers can make of such information. Investigators found that teachers who had access to information about how children are likely to solve addition and subtraction word problems of various kinds were more likely than teachers who did not have this information to select and create a wider variety of word problems and to focus more on the methods children invented to solve the problems (Carpenter et al. 1989). In other words, teachers can use their knowledge of students' thinking to select and design appropriate tasks and to use them wisely.

Constructing conceptual maps of the subject and learning about students' thinking are not trivial tasks. Teachers face a real challenge in acquiring this knowledge. But we believe it is the kind of knowledge that should provide the target for teachers and the kind of knowledge that teachers can build over time. Teachers can build their knowledge of students' thinking by reading the available literature and by listening to their own students solving problems and sharing strategies. Over time, teachers can accumulate a wealth of information about how their students are likely to solve problems, and about what kind of residue different problems are likely to leave behind.

Providing Relevant Information

How much information should teachers provide? How much should teachers tell students? These questions have been discussed for years. Traditional practice has been to provide lots of information. In fact, teaching has, at times, become synonymous with presenting information; good teaching has often been synonymous with presenting information clearly. Periodically, educational reformers have advocated presenting less information, shifting more responsibility to the students to search for or invent the information they need.

Early in this century, John Dewey (1910) recognized the importance of this question. He said that no educational question was more important than how we can learn from what others tell us. If teachers tell too much, students will not need to develop their own problem-solving abilities; if teachers tell too little, students will not make much progress. Nearly twenty-five years later, Dewey saw that this question was still plaguing teachers. Some teachers said they were following Dewey's proposals by withholding information from students and allowing students to discover and invent things on their own. Dewey (1933) attempted to clarify his position by saying that teachers should provide information if it is needed for students to continue their problem-solving efforts and they cannot readily find it themselves, and if it is presented as something to consider and not as a prescription to follow. Dewey then said, "Provided the student is genuinely engaged upon a topic, and provided the teacher is willing to give the student a good deal of leeway as to what he assimilates and retains (not requiring rigidly that everything be grasped or reproduced), there is comparatively little danger that one who is himself enthusiastic will communicate too much concerning a topic" (270).

How much information to share is at the heart of the dilemma identified earlier. We agree with Dewey that the teacher should feel free, and obligated, to share relevant information. Too much information is being shared only if it is interfering with opportunities for students to problematize mathematics. In other words, information can and should be shared as long as it does not solve the problem, does not take away the need for students to reflect on the situation and develop solution methods that they understand.

Sharing Mathematical Conventions

Teachers can provide several kinds of useful information: One is the conventions that are used in mathematics for recording and communicating actions and ideas. These include the names and written symbols for numbers, operations, and relationships (e.g., equality), and special terminology used in the wider mathematics community (e.g., words like quotient and variable, and formats for writing equations). These are social conventions and students cannot be expected to discover them. However, we often make the mistake of burdening students with these conventions, rather than providing them as beneficial aids. Rather than presenting them as things to be memorized, they should be shared when they can be used by students to record what they already know and communicate it to others. This issue will be taken up again in Chapter 5.

Sharing Alternative Methods

A second kind of information that teachers can provide could be called suggestions for helping students improve their methods of solution. In order to assist students without interfering, we can suggest the following guidelines based on our experience. First, it is usually *not* a good a idea to recommend that students change their own methods to bring them more in line with the standard algorithms. For example, if a student is adding 17 + 54 by adding 10 and 50 to get 60, then adding 7 and 4 to get 11, and then adding 60 and 11 to get 71, we would advise against saying, "Why don't you start with the ones and then add the extra ten to the tens?" Such suggestions can easily be interpreted by students as critiques on the deficiencies of their methods and requests to follow the teacher's method. Students then shift their focus from reflecting on mathematics to searching for what the teacher wants.

Teachers can enter the discussion by suggesting an alternative method to the methods shared by the students. If students are struggling with cumbersome or flawed methods, a teacher's suggestion can invigorate the discussion and move it forward. If done carefully, students can accept the teacher's method as another method to consider and analyze. There can be a problem, however, if students receive the teacher's presentation as a preferred method simply because the teacher presented it. The bottom line is why students are choosing particular methods. Students should use methods because they understand them and can defend them, not because they feel obligated to use them or to please the teacher. Methods should be preferred based on their merits as discussed in class, not based on who presented them.

Another way in which teachers can help students improve their methods is by suggesting more efficient or clearer recording techniques. When students work through solutions on paper, they can develop quite cumbersome and confusing notation. Without changing their methods, teachers can suggest recording techniques that would be easier for everyone to understand. This is part of helping students communicate their methods to others.

Articulating Ideas in Students' Methods

A third kind of information that teachers can, and should, share with students is the way in which students' methods capture powerful ideas in mathematics. Students can invent appropriate methods for solving problems without being aware of all the ideas on which the methods are built. Helping students reflect on these ideas by pointing them out can be empowering for students. For example, a very common method that students develop for adding mulitdigit numbers is to decompose them into tens and ones, combine like units, and then recombine them. This kind of transformation is, in general terms, an extremely powerful method and reveals important properties of numbers (and all mathematical expressions). Indeed, we do all arithmetic by decomposing the quantities in some way so we can combine like units. Given an appropriate time and opportunity, it would be useful to initiate a discussion with students about this feature of their methods. In how many ways could the numbers be decomposed and recombined to yield the same result?

By restating and clarifying students' solution methods and the ideas on which they are built, teachers not only highlight the mathematical ideas, but also endow the method with some importance. By selecting certain methods for examination, teachers show that they value the methods or ideas. Teachers can use this to help guide students' attention toward particular ideas and relationships. This provides teachers with a powerful way to direct the mathematics that is encountered in the classroom. But teachers must also be aware that students can misinterpret a teacher's clarification of a method as instructions to abandon their own sense-making and follow the highlighted procedure. So, teachers need to be aware of these possibilities and guard against misinterpretations. This is simply part of the dilemma for teachers identified earlier.

Summary

When thinking about how to guide the mathematical activities of the class, teachers are always faced with a dilemma: how to support students as thinkers and creative problem solvers and how to help them learn important mathematics. These dual aims can create real tensions. The system of instruction we are describing deals with the dilemma by asking the teacher to accept two responsibilities: selecting appropriate tasks and providing relevant information. Neither of these are easy because they need to be carried out with an appreciation for both sides of the dilemma and a deep knowledge of the subject and the student. But both responsibilities provide ways for teachers to treat the dilemma as a positive force and deal with it constructively.

Guiding the Development of Classroom Culture

The second major role for the teacher is to establish the kind of environment or culture in the classroom that supports reflection and communication. This means establishing a classroom culture that treats tasks as genuine mathematical problems. We will discuss the social aspects of such an environment in the next chapter. In this section we focus on what the teacher must do to guide the development of the culture. We will highlight two responsibilities: One is to focus the mathematical attention on methods of solving problems. The second is for the teacher to make clear (to herself or himself and to the students) in what sense she or he is an authority.

Focus on Methods

We borrow again from John Dewey (1929) who pointed out that the central feature of communities that work together to investigate a subject and seek to understand it is a focus on methods used to solve problems. The methods used by different individuals should be open for examination, and discussion, and the goal of all participants should be to search for better methods. No one should be tied too closely to their own method, but should be looking for ways to improve it. Engaging in open, honest, public discussions of methods is the best way to gain deeper understandings of the subject.

Similarly, classroom mathematics discussions should be about sharing, analyzing, and improving methods of solving problems. The teacher must take the lead in directing students' communications toward conversations about methods. This means that students must first be allowed and encouraged to develop their own methods of solution. For example, suppose second graders have just been solving 53 − 18. A good deal of class time should be devoted to students sharing methods of solution, clarifying their descriptions so everyone understands, and comparing different methods. Preferences for particular methods should be elicited and discussed. Students should retain the option of choosing their own method, but everyone should share the goal of searching for the method that works best for them.

Focusing the discussions on methods has both intellectual and social purposes: Intellectually, it is the best way of focusing students' attention on what is mathematically important and encouraging them to reflect on mathematical relationships. Such activity is essential for building understanding. Socially, it establishes a common goal toward which everyone can work and to which all can contribute. The analysis of all methods, both flawed and appropriate, contributes to finding better methods. In addition, discussions of methods focus attention on ideas rather than people. Features of methods, not their presenters, become the currency of the classroom. Of course, this kind of shared culture is not developed automatically (Lampert et al. in press). Teachers must work carefully and over time to lead the class toward such a culture.

Adopt Appropriate Position of Authority

Teachers have numerous responsibilities in the classroom that place them in positions of authority. They are, of course, responsible for the safety and general welfare of the students while in the classroom and they become the authority on these matters. They also are responsible for many managerial aspects of the class and must assume an authoritative role to carry out some of these responsibilities. With regard to both the mathematical and social aspects of classroom life, the question of authority does not have a simple answer. As we argued in the previous sections, teachers are responsible for guiding the mathematical activities of the class and for establishing the tone and focus of classroom interactions. However, these responsibilities must be discharged with a continuing sensitivity for the autonomy of students' intellectual activity. Authority, in these cases, does not mean unilateral imposition. It means taking the initiative to work with students toward a shared goal.

There are some areas in which teachers should explicitly remove themselves from a position of authority, one of which is deciding whether answers are correct. In traditional systems of instruction, teachers are asked to provide feedback on students' responses, to tell them whether or not they are right. In the system we are describing, this is almost always unnecessary and usually inappropriate. Mathematics is a unique subject because there is often only one right answer, and because correctness is not a matter of opinion; it is built into the logic and structure of the subject. In other words, everyone will agree on the right answer to a problem if they understand the problem and think about it long enough. Part of what it means to understand mathematics is to understand the problem and the method used to solve it. When this happens, the solver knows whether the answer is correct. There is no need for the teacher to have the final word on correctness. The final word is provided by the logic of the subject and the students' explanations and justifications that are built on this logic.

Many teachers worry that if they do not step in when a wrong answer is given or a flawed method is presented, students will be led astray and develop misunderstandings. Our experience is if the tasks are appropriately challenging, that is, if they link up with students' thinking and allow students to use familiar tools, and if there is full discussion of various solution methods and solutions by the students after they have completed the task, then sound mathematical thinking and correct solutions eventually carry the day. Inappropriate methods rarely go unchallenged by other students; the most convincing arguments are those that make mathematical sense.

A change from traditional instruction in the locus of authority in this area has profound ramifications throughout the system. If teachers remove themselves from adjudicating correctness of solutions, students will be more inclined to look to their own arguments to decide on correctness. They will be free to develop confidence in their own methods and their own monitoring skills for deciding whether something makes sense. They will be less inclined to try to uncover what the teacher wants or to guess what the answer key says. They will be free to focus their attention on developing justifications for their methods and solutions based on the logic of mathematics.

Teachers Make the System Work

In the system of instruction we are describing, the teachers play an active and central role. They are responsible for guiding the mathematical activities of students and for establishing a classroom culture in which students reflect on and communicate about mathematics. For the system to work, teachers must act on these responsibilities in ways that honor students as thinkers and mathematics as a discipline. Although this is not easy, we believe it provides the right target toward which we should be moving.

4 *The Social Culture of the Classroom*

For some readers, including the social culture as an essential dimension of the mathematics classroom may seem curious. Tasks (Chapter 2) and teachers (Chapter 3) make obvious contributions to students' learning, but is the social environment so important? The answer is yes, and the reasons should become clear in this chapter. We stated earlier that the key processes in building understanding are reflection and communication. To this point we have emphasized reflection and the construction of mathematics by each student. Now we turn our attention to communication and the means by which students build mathematics together.

Benefits of a Healthy Social Culture

Doing mathematics as part of a group means seeing yourself as a participant of a community. Communities share certain goals and certain ways of working together toward the goals. In mathematics communities, the goals are problems to be solved and understandings to be developed. The ways of working together are norms for communicating and interacting with each other. Learning to be a member of a mathematical community means taking ownership of the goals and accepting the norms of social interaction. Why is it important that classrooms become mathematical communities and that all students participate? Because such communities provide rich environments for developing deep understandings of mathematics.

We believe that the opportunities for building mathematical understandings are enhanced when students work together to solve problems and interact intensively about solution methods. We have included several kinds of the most important benefits here.

Doing Mathematics Involves Collaboration

Our descriptions of doing mathematics have centered around solving genuine mathematical problems. Observations of how mathematical communities solve problems show both individual and group efforts. Group efforts require a great deal of communication. Assumptions about what things mean must be agreed on, assertions or conjectures are made, methods of solutions are proposed and defended, challenges are usually offered, and discussions are held about the soundness and accuracy of solutions. These activities are all part of doing mathematics and all involve intensive communication and social interaction. Classrooms that experience some form of these activities reveal to their participants what doing mathematics is all about.

Traditional forms of instruction often encourage, and even require, students to work alone. Working together or using the suggestions of a peer have been discouraged. Students are suppose to do their own work and not rely on others. This concern may result, in part, from the importance that has been placed on assessing individual student's abilities and performance. We believe this concern, which has sometimes become an obsession, has had a destructive effect on the climate and culture of mathematics classrooms. It is a concern that has exceeded its appropriate boundaries and has turned classrooms into artificial environments that undermine students' attempts to do mathematics. Doing mathematics is a collaborative activity. It depends on communication and social interaction.

Communication Makes Information and Solution Methods Available

When students are working on their own, they can get locked into thinking of a problem in only one way, and developing only one method of solving it. When students work together to search for better methods, they each share their own methods and listen to those of others. This is likely to place a variety of methods on the table. Through discussing the methods and comparing the advantages of each, students can lift themselves out of their rut and see the problem in a new way. Students can increase their understanding of the problem and of different methods that work.

A third-grade class was working on the following problem: Bugs Bunny has 75 carrots. If he eats 5 carrots each day, for how many days does he have food? Most students solved the problem by writing 5s until they reached 75 and then counting the number of 5s. Maria solved the problem by writing $10 \times 5 = 50$, $5 \times 5 = 25$, and $10 + 5 = 15$. After the different methods had been presented, the class discussed the ways in which Maria's method was different from the others. Some students decided it was basically the same because Maria had added fives too, just in groups. The teacher then asked Maria why she chose 10 fives to start and not, say, 7 fives. Maria said she knew the answer to 10×5 so it was easy. This class discussion may look rather innocuous, but it had a significant effect on the way many students thought about division. After the discussion, a number of students began division problems by looking for multiples of the divisor, often choosing multiples or powers of 10. These were important breakthroughs in students' understandings and in the development of better methods.

Our belief that working together in this way is more productive for students than working alone is supported by the available evidence. After reviewing research studies that investigated students' learning during cooperative or group problem solving activities versus competitive or individual problem-solving activities, Qin et al. (1995) concluded that cooperative settings are more beneficial for students' learning. They suggested, as do we, that a major reason for this may be that students are exposed to a greater variety of methods and have more chances to talk about why they work.

In addition to introducing more methods into the discussion and analyzing them more deeply, peer interaction places challenging problems within reach. By working together, students can share information and pool expertise, and thereby help each other work through new problems and develop new methods of solution. Students can solve problems and construct understandings working collaboratively that they would not be able to accomplish working alone (Noddings 1985; Schoenfeld 1989). Different students point out different relationships, different aspects of the problem, different approaches for solving problems. Things get noticed that might otherwise have been ignored. New kinds of understandings become possible.

Communication in the classroom also can help make implicit ideas explicit. Often students come to school with intuitive ideas about how things work, and intuitive strategies for solving problems. Sometimes they can solve problems and not be able to express clearly how they solved them. By encouraging students to share and discuss methods of solution, they have the chance to clarify their ideas—for themselves and for others. When students' intuitive strategies are made public, they can be analyzed more deeply and everyone can learn from them.

We suggested in Chapter 3 that teachers can help to make explicit important ideas in students' methods that might be used intuitively and might go unnoticed. We used the example of adding two-digit numbers by decomposing them into tens and ones, adding the tens together and the ones together, and then recombining them. Students, as well as teachers, can play the role of making implicit ideas explicit by engaging in discussions about why methods work and whether they would work on other problems. For example, students can learn to think about and ask questions like, would decomposition work for all addition problems, regardless of the size of the numbers? Would decomposition work for subtraction? The reconsideration of methods that is needed to deal with these questions leaves behind new insights and deep understandings.

Creating Cognitive Conflict

cognitive dissonance

Since Piaget's ground-breaking work we have known that we all improve our own thinking as our ideas are challenged and we reevaluate our points of view. The conflict we sense should not come from outside pressure, but from an internal dissonance: Something is not settled. We realize that our ideas did not make as much sense as we thought, and that other ways of thinking would be more satisfying. This kind of conflict is created by communicating with others.

In mathematics class, cognitive conflict is created as students present their ideas and solution methods, defend them in the face of questions, and question others' ideas. These experiences encourage students to deal with incongruities, to reevaluate their methods, to elaborate, clarify, and reorganize their own thinking. Peer interaction is especially helpful because the differences in thinking are likely to be within a range that will generate genuine, fruitful conflict. Students often challenge each other in ways that they can make sense of and deal with productively (Doise and Mugny 1984).

Norms of a Healthy Social Culture

The benefits of a social community in the mathematics classroom do not happen automatically (Lampert et al. in press; Salomon and Globerson 1989). Students do not always share the same goals, nor are they always mindful of the feelings and needs of others. Building a community of mathematical practice requires teachers to take the lead in establishing appropriate expectations and norms. There are four guidelines we can identify. The guidelines build on and elaborate the recommendations identified in Chapter 1 and described near the end of Chapter 3.

Discussions Are About Methods and Ideas

The focus of classroom interactions should be about methods for solving problems. The goal of the interactions should be to improve the methods, to make them more powerful and more efficient. This achieves two objectives: First, it places the attention on what is most likely to facilitate students' understandings. Second, it directs attention away from personal issues that can derail the discussions and undermine the group's attempts to establish a healthy supportive environment.

As we have stated many times, students are most likely to build important mathematical understandings as they develop and analyze methods for solving problems. What is equally true is that examining carefully someone's ideas and solution methods is one of the best ways to show respect, both for the ideas and for their author. Ideas and methods expressed by all participants deserve respect, not only because they can contribute to everyone's learning, but because such respect is the foundation on which to build healthy social interactions.

Students Choose Their Own Methods and Share Them with Others

A familiar refrain in this book is that students should develop their own solution methods. As teachers allow and encourage students to work out their own methods, the opportunities for students to construct important mathematical understandings increase. But honoring students' autonomy to choose methods is about more than opportunities to reflect on mathematics: It is about developing communication and social interaction patterns that will support such reflection in the long run. And this requires that teachers and students share the responsibility.

The teacher must help students to recognize that they are expected to understand the methods they use and to help others understand them. A student's responsibility does not end when she or he has used a method successfully. The student must then work out a way to present and explain the method so others understand. Lampert (in press) suggested that an alternative definition of understanding could be "to make yourself understood." In other words, I can claim to understand a method if I can help others understand it. Teachers need to help students accept the responsibility to do just that.

Students also must respect each other's need to understand the methods that are used. Not every student will be persuaded by every argument; however, there are a variety of methods that will work. This allows each student to feel in control of his or her work. Furthermore, it creates an openness and collaborative atmosphere that is essential for building a community that is working together to improve solution methods and construct understandings.

A related responsibility for students is to recognize that learning means learning from others, taking advantage of others' ideas and the results of their problem-solving activity, and putting the received information to good use. This does not mean that students wait for others to do the work and steal their methods. The first part of each student's responsibility is to share methods she or he understands. But not all methods will be invented by all students. In a healthy community, there will be a good deal of give and take and students will learn from each other. This means that students will need to listen. We have in mind here more than listening out of politeness or respect, but also be-cause of a genuine interest in what the speaker has to say (Paley 1986). Students will then need to use the new information appropriately. Full participants in a community of mathematical practice are good listeners and wise users.

As we learn more about students' interactions, we are finding that the benefits occur in just these situations—where both the sharer and the receiver are actively involved in communicating. For example, Webb et al. (1995) reported that seventh graders learned more mathematics if students shared explanations, not just simple prescriptions or right an-swers, and if the receivers acted on the information in some way, such as using it to help solve another problem. Participants had to work to share useful information, to make themselves understood, and to use the new information constructively. These are significant responsibilities, and stu-dents must learn to take ownership of them.

Mistakes Are Sites for Learning

If students are encouraged to develop their own solution methods they will develop and present methods that sometimes are mathematically flawed. How should teachers handle these situations? Many teachers are concerned about this, and see it as an unfortunate consequence of relin-quishing control over the methods students use. This is a serious issue, because if teachers view students' mistakes only in a negative way and try to prevent them, the system of instruction we are describing will col-lapse. As soon as we try to prevent students from making mistakes, we begin specifying the methods they should use. This removes the prob-lematic nature of the task—the foundations of the system.

Fortunately, there is another way of viewing students' mistakes. The view is made possible by recalling that the goal of mathematics in-struction is to help students construct deep understandings, and achieving this goal is a natural outcome of resolving problems by re-flecting on them and communicating about them. These processes work as students develop and improve methods of solution. And im-proving methods of solution means moving from methods that do not work as well, and even may be flawed, toward methods that work bet-ter. Making mistakes is a natural part of this process; it even may be essential sometimes. Mistakes simply are outcomes of methods that need to be improved. Mistakes, if treated appropriately, can contribute to everyone's understanding. It is important to see that this view is not just trying to put a good face on a bad situation: It is claiming that mis-takes are a natural and important part of the process of improving methods of solution and should play a constructive role in classroom discussions.

Establishing the constructive role that mistakes can play goes a long way toward building a healthy social culture. If students are to engage seriously in doing mathematics, they need an intellectual and social safe place. They need an environment where they are free to take risks, to experiment, to try things out without being ridiculed. They need to feel that their thoughts can contribute to the classroom enterprise, even if they are not entirely correct.

Setting this norm is not an easy task for the teachers or the students (Lampert et al. in press). Students must feel free to contribute, but not become weary of having their inner thoughts continually exposed and challenged. Teachers need to set a balanced tone. They should welcome students' suggestions, whether correct or incorrect, as potentially valuable opportunities for discussion and analysis. Covering for students who offer incorrect suggestions, or applauding them, both convey that there is something unnatural about the suggestion. A better approach is simply to reflect the suggestion back to the class for discussion, with the explicit aim of learning something new, seeing something that has remained hidden until now. Summarizing or affirming what was learned by discussing a particular error can emphasize how one can learn from mistakes.

Correctness Is Determined by the Logic of Mathematics

A fourth guideline for setting social norms is the recognition that the correctness of methods and solutions can and should be determined by the logic of the subject, rather than the teacher or a popular student. The responsibility for setting this norm also must be shared by the teacher and students. We concluded Chapter 3 by describing the responsibility of teachers in removing themselves from positions of authority in this regard. Teachers also must help students see that they can, over time and collectively, determine correctness by relying on their own arguments.

Students must learn to live with some uncertainty as they evaluate the mathematical sense of a proposed method and solution. Debates about correctness may take time and require further examination and investigation. Holding correctness in suspension while the discussion and investigation continue runs counter to most practices in which teachers provide immediate feedback. But, as Dewey (1929, 1933) strongly argued, experiencing this kind of uncertainty and even learning to enjoy it is an essential part of thoughtful problem solving.

For students to accept the responsibility of determining correctness and managing temporary uncertainties, they must develop confidence in themselves and their peers as capable sense-makers. Actually, the acceptance of responsibility and the development of confidence probably develop together, both feeding off each other. But for the process to work, students must learn to rely on the group—as much as themselves—to evaluate whether things make sense. This creates a significant interdependency between the individual student and the class. Every student needs the class and the class needs each student. A healthy social culture is the result.

An illustration of how this can work is provided by a fourth-grade class that was working on the problem $\frac{1}{4} + \frac{1}{3}$. Some students were working with pencil and paper, some were drawing diagrams and shading parts of objects, and some were working with sets of fraction pieces they had made previously. After they had been working about ten minutes, most of them had developed a method and reached a solution. The first student to present showed that $\frac{1}{4} + \frac{1}{3} = \frac{2}{7}$ by demonstrating a written method. The student explained that it is easiest to just add the top numbers and the bottom numbers. Teachers will recognize this as a common error. Many teachers feel obligated to step in and correct the student, saying that you cannot add the numerators unless the denominators are the same. The teacher in this class thanked the student for the presentation and asked if there were any questions or if other students had used different methods. Several students said they had used fraction pieces and they weren't sure of the exact answer but it was much more than $\frac{2}{7}$. They argued that $\frac{2}{7}$ could not be the answer because when you combine $\frac{1}{3}$ and $\frac{1}{4}$, you have to get more than $\frac{1}{2}$. The students who drew diagrams agreed that the answer was larger than $\frac{2}{7}$, but there was no consensus about the exact answer. The teacher asked what they would need to find the answer, and they recalled the kinds of addition problems on which they previously had found exact answers (denominators were the same). The students went back to work but at the end of the lesson had not yet reached a clear conclusion. The activity was continued the next day.

This example shows students taking over the responsibility for determining correctness by questioning peers' solutions, using reasonableness as a guide, and living with temporary uncertainty. If the teacher had immediately corrected the proposed solution of $\frac{2}{7}$, the culture of the classroom would have changed. It is likely that students would have shifted their goals from finding the solution by making sense of the mathematics to searching for the teacher's method.

Some Things Are Optional

We believe the four norms we have described are essential for creating a classroom culture that encourages reflection and communication about mathematics. There are other aspects of the classroom, often discussed as part of the social environment, that we believe are optional. For example, much has been written recently about grouping within the class (for a review see Good et al. 1992). Some advocate using small groups, some suggest particular compositions of groups. The system of instruction we are describing works well with a variety of grouping arrangements. Students can work in small groups or by themselves. Discussions can take place within groups or as a whole class. Our experience suggests that it is useful to allow some time for students to work quietly, on their own, and some time for whole class discussions of methods. But the exact nature of the grouping arrangements should be left to the preference of the teacher and the needs of the particular class.

Social Culture as Part of the System

Although we have identified five dimensions that make up a system of instruction and have separated them for discussion, it is important to remember that they are fully mixed and entangled in practice. In fact, that is what a *system* means.

We can now illustrate one critical way in which the dimensions work together. We noted in Chapter 2 that reflecting on mathematics in a way that leads to understanding depends on encountering tasks that invite reflection, tasks that provide something interesting and intriguing and perplexing on which to reflect. In other words, a critical feature of Dimension 1 is that tasks must allow students to treat the mathematics as problematic. We also noted, however, that whether students do so does not depend only on the task. It requires, among other things, that students make it *their* goal to solve the problem. They must see the task as a challenge or perplexity that they would like to resolve.

What determines whether students set the goal of solving a problem or resolving a perplexity? We believe that the answer is located mostly within Dimensions 2 and 3. The way in which students approach tasks will depend as much on the culture of the classroom as on the tasks themselves. Whether students adopt the goal of reflecting on the task, of noticing its nuances and complexities, or of wanting to find a reasonable solution, will depend largely on the expectations that have developed in the classroom. Tasks that are designed to be appropriately problematic for students may be changed by students or teachers, as they are implemented, into low-level conventional exercises (Stein et al. 1996). This, in turn may limit the kinds of residues that students take with them from the activity (Saxe et al. 1996; Stein and Lane in press). How students are expected to deal with mathematical tasks is negotiated by the teacher (Dimension 2) and the students (Dimension 3) as they establish the culture of the classroom (Ball 1993a; Cobb et al. 1992; Fennema et al. 1992).

Even routine-looking tasks, such as 45 + 38 or $\frac{1}{3}$ + $\frac{1}{4}$ can be problematized by students, and can provide the source for rich problem solving if they are presented at the appropriate time and if the culture of the class encourages students to treat them problematically. On the other hand, even large-scale real-life problems can be drained of their problematic possibilities if the culture of the class encourages students to wait for demonstrations of how to solve such problems and then mimic what they have seen.

So, in order for the critical features of Dimensions 1 and 2 to be realized, the social culture of the classroom (Dimension 3) must fit comfortably with the rest of the system. In order for students to have opportunities to reflect on and communicate about mathematics, the classroom dimensions must work closely together.

5 *Mathematical Tools as Learning Supports*

The fourth dimension of classrooms that has important consequences for the development of understanding is the kind of mathematical tools that are available. In Chapter 2 we defined tools broadly to include oral language, physical materials, written symbols, and skills students already have acquired. In this chapter we will focus our attention on the first three kinds of tools: language, materials, and symbols. These tools can be introduced into the classroom environment, by the teacher or students, as external supports for learning. They should be thought of as "amplifiers of human capacities" (Bruner 1966, 81). Tools should help students do things more easily or help students do things they could not do alone.

Tools can be used in a number of ways to amplify students' mathematical activity. They can provide a convenient and permanent record of mathematical activity. If students want to remember a particular quantity or action, they can represent it with words or materials or symbols and then use this record later to recall the activity. Tools can also provide a way of communicating with others. Words, of course, are a primary communication tool, but materials and written symbols also can be used effectively in this way. Finally, tools can be used to think with. They can make difficult thoughts easier to manage; they can enable some thoughts that would hardly be possible without them; and they can shape the kinds of thoughts we have.

We will explore each of these uses in this chapter. But before we begin these discussions, we should consider the question of how it is that students make sense of tools. How do students develop meaning for tools?

Developing Meaning for Tools

How students construct meaning for tools in the mathematics classroom is a very complicated question. For starters, tools play a kind of intermediary role in the development of meaning. In order for students to use tools wisely, they need to develop meaning for the tools. Once some meaning is established, the tools can be used to solve problems and to help students develop meaning for other things. At this point, tools become real supports for learning.

Another complication is that the meaning that students construct for a tool is likely to depend on the purpose for which it is being used. Students can use physical materials, for example, as tools for generating answers, perhaps as calculation devices; or they can use the materials as tools for reflecting on how and why things work. Depending on the goal that teachers and students set, different meanings for the tool will emerge.

Meaning Must Be Constructed for and with Tools

Consider the numeral 32. These marks on paper can become useful tools for students. But they do not come with meaning and will not automatically be used effectively, just as a metal file does not come with meaning and will not automatically be used effectively. The meaning must be constructed by the user. This happens by examining the tool carefully, trying it out in different contexts, and listening to what it means to other people. Once a tool user has become familiar with the metal file, it can be used effectively to sharpen a variety of objects and to develop deeper knowledge of the objects, such as the relative softness of different metals. Once a student has constructed meaning for 32, the numeral can be used as a tool for constructing deeper meanings for other mathematical objects, such as other numerals and operations, like addition and subtraction.

Students must construct meaning for all tools, even those that may look obvious to adults. For years teachers have used physical materials, such as base-ten blocks, to show the meanings of numerals, like 32. But base-ten blocks are just tools. The blocks do not automatically have meaning for students. Meaning must be constructed by interacting with the blocks (not by watching demonstrations). As the blocks begin to mean something, they can be used as tools for constructing meanings for other representations, such as the numeral 32, and for solving a variety of problems.

One thing that makes this process very complicated is that meaning for and with tools does not happen in a neat order. One does not construct complete meaning for a tool and then use the tool to help develop meaning for something else. It seems to be more mixed up than this and goes back and forth. As you use a tool, you get to know the tool better and you use the tool more effectively to help you know about other things.

So, there are two points to keep in mind as we discuss the uses of classroom mathematics tools: First, meaning is not inherent in the tool; students construct meaning for it. We cannot assume that tools immediately have meaning for students, regardless of how obvious the meaning appears to us. Second, meaning developed *for* tools and meaning developed *with* tools both result from actively *using* tools. Teachers do not need to provide long demonstrations before allowing students to use tools; teachers just need to be aware that when students are using tools they are working on two fronts simultaneously: what the tool means and how it can be used effectively to understand something else.

Different Kinds of Meanings Can Be Developed

Allowing students to use tools does not guarantee that all students will develop the same meanings for them. Students who use tools as aids for calculating answers are likely to develop different meanings than students who use them to explore alternative solution methods or reflect on the reasons the methods work.

An example that shows the difference between using tools to generate answers and using them to think about the logic of the solution method is provided by a fourth-grade class that was adding fractions with unlike denominators for the first time. The teacher demonstrated how to draw pictures of the fractions (a rectangle cut into parts) and then suggested using the pictures to find the answer. Students were given the problem $\frac{1}{2} + \frac{1}{4}$. Some students drew two rectangles and shaded $\frac{1}{2}$ of one and $\frac{1}{4}$ of the other. They counted the number of shaded parts and the total number of parts, and wrote $\frac{2}{6}$ as the answer. Other students drew the same two rectangles, partitioned both of them into fourths, shaded $\frac{1}{4}$ of one rectangle and $\frac{1}{2}$ of the other, counted up the shaded parts and the total number of parts, and wrote $\frac{3}{8}$ as the answer. Still other students drew one rectangle, shaded $\frac{1}{2}$ of it, partitioned the other half into fourths and shaded $\frac{1}{4}$, noticed that $\frac{1}{4}$ was left unshaded, and wrote $\frac{3}{4}$ as the answer.

At this point in the lesson students had developed some meaning for the tool, but the meaning was based on using the tool as a physical calculation device. The same errors were produced by these students manipulating the drawings as are often produced when students manipulate the written symbols. Even students who wrote $\frac{3}{4}$ had not used the tool to reflect on *why* $\frac{1}{2} + \frac{1}{4} = \frac{3}{4}$.

As the class discussion proceeded, the teacher and students examined the different solution methods, constructed some additional drawings to show $\frac{1}{6} + \frac{1}{6}$ and $\frac{1}{8} + \frac{2}{8}$, compared these with the earlier drawings, and noticed the importance of the unit when using these drawings as a tool. What unit is implied when writing $\frac{1}{2} + \frac{1}{4}$, how to make drawings consistent with this meaning, and how to partition the drawing so one can easily determine the result became the focal points of the discussion. It was during this discussion, when the purpose of using the tool shifted from just finding an answer to examining the problem situation and reflecting on the alternative methods of solution, that students began constructing deeper meanings for the tool, and deeper meanings for fraction addition.

We have often oversimplified the way in which tools can help students learn mathematics with understanding. Teachers have been told that, for example, to prevent students from making silly errors when adding fractions, such as $\frac{1}{2} + \frac{1}{4} = \frac{2}{6}$, they just need to provide some materials, such as fraction pieces or fraction drawings. These tools, some have said, will ensure that students develop meaning for fractions and add fractions correctly. As we have seen, and as many teachers know, it is not that simple. Tools can be extremely helpful, but it matters how the tools are used and for what purpose. In the next section, we explore several different purposes for which mathematical tools might be used.

Using Tools

Using Tools to Keep Records

Some tools can be used to keep convenient and semipermanent records of mathematical activity. Such records can be used for marking an action in shorthand, remembering a partial result when solving a problem, recalling what was done on a previous problem, picking up where one left off, and so on. We have observed some teachers using students' invented recording systems or introducing informal recording methods that students have readily adopted. Some students have used an arrow notation to record the steps in their arithmetic calculations. Here is what one student wrote as she added 18 + 23:

$$10 + 20 \rightarrow 30 + 8 \rightarrow 38 + 3 \rightarrow 41$$

This record shows that she added the tens in the 18 and the 23. Then she added the 8 to get 38, and then she added on the 3 to get the answer, 41.

The arrow notation allowed the student to keep a running record of the partial sums and the operations on them. Arrows are used instead of equal signs because the answers keep getting built up and, as a consequence, the respective terms are not equal. So, using the equal sign here either would result in incorrect expressions or would constrain students' actions. The arrows fit more easily with the students' adding methods. Also, using the arrow notation here allows the correct meaning for the equal sign, = , to be developed in other contexts.

Standard written symbols may not fit children's actions as easily because they have been streamlined over hundreds of years to contain a maximum amount of information with a minimum amount of writing. This means they are quite dense and students can find it difficult to construct meaning for them. Nevertheless, record keeping may still be the best way to introduce standard written symbols. That is, the standard written symbols should be introduced by the teacher as a way of recording something that students have already done or already know.

A first-grade class in early spring had been solving story problems using physical materials, drawings, and a variety of counting strategies. Now they wanted to keep track of the results of their work. The story they just solved was "Maria had 17 medals but lost 9 when her family moved to a new house. How many medals does Maria have now?" Students suggested a variety of ways they could keep a record of this problem. The teacher introduced $17 - 9 = 8$ as one way of keeping track, and the class discussed how this represented the story. Students liked how quickly they could write this representation and began using number sentences as records of stories that they solved.

The example illustrates using standard symbols as records of things that students already know. The experiences that are represented by the symbols provide anchors for the symbols. Students can tie the symbols to something that already has meaning for them. We have found that when standard written symbols are introduced in this way, students can develop appropriate meanings for the symbols and then begin using the symbols effectively as tools for solving problems. This is true both for young students, like the first graders in the example (Bebout 1990; Carpenter et al. 1988), and for older students when they begin working with a new notation system, such as decimal fractions (Wearne and Hiebert 1988a, 1988b).

Using Tools to Communicate

As we have noted many times, communication is a hallmark of classrooms in which students build mathematical understandings. Oral language, materials, and written symbols all can be used as tools for communication. Everyone is aware of the importance of language for communication, but how about materials and symbols? How can they be used to improve communication?

A fourth-grade class was adding decimal fractions for the first time. The students had been talking about decimal fraction quantities for several days and had been using base-ten blocks to represent the quantities. One student related that the gasoline can at home for filling the lawn mower held two and four-tenths gallons of gas. Students represented this amount with the base-ten blocks in a variety of ways, using different size blocks for the unit and different groupings (2 flats and 4 sticks [flat is one], 2 sticks and 4 small cubes [stick is one], 1 stick and 14 small cubes, and so on). When the teacher posed the first arithmetic problem (How much gasoline would we have if we combined two and four-tenths gallons from Hilda's can and one and eight-tenths gallons from Neil's can? Would we have enough to fill a tractor mower that held four and one-half gallons?) students represented each quantity with the blocks, joined them together, and worked out the total. As students presented their methods, they described them with words and showed them with blocks. The blocks provided a focal point for the presentations. Everyone looked at the blocks, commented on them, and asked questions about them. They provided a referent for the communication. They kept everyone's attention focused in the same place. This is one way that materials can facilitate effective communication. Everyone can be talking about and thinking about more or less the same thing.

An important consequence of communicating clearly, of using a referent that focuses everyone's attention, is that students develop *shared* understandings. If students just work individually they can develop different conceptions of important mathematical entities, such as decimal fractions. When students interact with each other, they notice differences and begin to negotiate them (Cobb et al. 1992). If they have something to point to, a referent to which they can all focus their attention, they can work toward clearer, better articulated, and more widely shared understandings.

When using words, materials, and symbols to keep records and to communicate, it becomes clear that there are important correspondences between them. In some sense, all three forms are capable of representing the same mathematical information. The simplest example is that a number can be represented with words (thirty-two), materials (3 bars of 10 unifix cubes and 2 extras), and symbols (32). One might conclude that the tools can be used interchangeably. In some ways this is true, but it is not the whole story. The different tools are different forms of representation, and each conveys a somewhat different message, and each emphasizes somewhat different features of the idea. Recognizing the similarities and differences between the forms is both an important and challenging task for students. It is important because creating relationships between forms is, in of itself, an avenue toward understanding. It is challenging because the relationships are subtle and complex.

Consider again the simple example of 32. The English number words are filled with irregularities and do not explicitly convey the structure of 3 tens and 2 ones. The problem is even worse with numbers like 12 or 18. It is not trivial for students to work out the relationships between the oral language and the written symbols for numbers (Fuson and Kwon 1991). Without such relationships the tools cannot be used as effectively for communicating. More than that, numbers themselves have less meaning. There is no easy and quick solution. Building relationships between forms of representation takes time and requires a good deal of discussion and reflection.

Using Tools to Think

The noted psychologist Vygotsky (1962, 1978) argued convincingly that our thoughts are influenced by the kinds of tools that we use. Although we might accept this statement at some level, we often do not appreciate its significance. We can see that when we perform physical tasks, such as gardening or brushing our teeth, how we deal with the task and whether we succeed are both influenced by the tools we use. But we do not always recognize that tools also can influence how we perform mental tasks, how we think about them, and whether we complete them successfully. In the remainder of the chapter, we will highlight several ways in which tools can serve as supports for thinking.

Connecting Current Activity with Past Experience

When students use old familiar tools to solve new problems, the tools help students connect the new activity with what they have done before. This is an important way in which we all make sense of things. Consider a classroom of third graders who had been using base-ten blocks to add and subtract large whole numbers. When they began examining numbers less than 1 they found that they could represent tenths, hundredths, and so on if they changed which block counted as the unit. When the large block was the unit, two flats showed two-tenths, six sticks showed six-hundredths, and so on. The principle of grouping by ten carried over from whole numbers and students used the blocks to capture this principle. Rather than confusing students, the same tool was used effectively to build relationships between what students already knew and what they were learning.

Extending Mental Capabilities

Thinking through some problems is extremely difficult. There are too many things to keep in mind at once. Consider the rather ordinary problem 26×578. Try to do it in your head. Human beings are notoriously bad at working through problems like this unless we have some help. We have developed many tools over the years to help us solve problems. Simple tools, such as written symbols arranged in certain ways, can help us solve the multiplication problem. We use tools like this so often that we do not fully appreciate them or recognize how dependent we are on them. Other tools, such as a calculator, now work well for this problem also.

A big advantage of using tools is that, in many cases, they can free our thinking for more creative activities. Written symbols have functioned for years in this way. Alfred North Whitehead (1948), the mathematician and philosopher, observed years ago that "By the aid of symbolism, we can make transitions in reasoning almost mechanically by the eye, which otherwise would call into play higher faculties of the brain. . . . By relieving the brain of all unnecessary work, a good notation sets it free to concentrate on more advanced problems" (39,41). New technologies provide new tools that can serve us even better in this way.

Shaping Our Thinking

In addition to helping us solve problems tools also shape the way we think about problems and influence the methods we develop for solving them. This is an especially important point for this book because it means that the tools students use influence the understandings that they construct. Students who use one set of tools may develop somewhat different understandings than students who use another set of tools. One kind of understanding is not necessarily better than another; they are just different. Teachers need to be aware of this so they can be sensitive to and appreciate the way in which the tools students use influence the kinds of methods developed and the kinds of understandings that are left behind. We will describe several examples to illustrate this point.

The first example comes from multidigit addition and subtraction. In order to appreciate the example, we need to describe briefly two different conceptions students can build for multidigit numbers (see Fuson et al. in press for a more complete account). One conception emphasizes the different units that are present in a multidigit number. The number 56, for example, is made up of 5 units of tens and 6 units of ones. The other conception emphasizes the way in which the number can be built from counting 10, 20, 30, 40, 50, 51, . . . 56. Young students who use base-ten blocks are likely to develop the units conception as an early and primary way of thinking about numbers (see the description of the CBI project in Chapter 8). Young students who engage in many counting activities using counting cards, hundreds charts, and so on, are likely to develop initially a counting conception of multidigit numbers (see the description of the PCL project in Chapter 9).

Given differences in the way students think about numbers, which is due, in part, to the differences in the tools they have used, there are likely to be differences in the methods they develop to add and subtract. Students who have a units conception are likely to add 34 and 51 by combining the 3 (tens) and 5 (tens) to get 8 (tens) and then combining the 4 (ones) and 1 (one) to get 5 (ones), for a total of 85. Students who have a counting conception are likely to count on from 51, perhaps 51, 61, 71, 81, 82, 83, 84, 85. Both methods are appropriate, but they signal different understandings. Of course, students may develop both conceptions, but the use of particular tools is likely to encourage particular conceptions as initial and favored points of view.

Our experience is echoed by Cobb et al. (in press). They report on their efforts to support first graders' attempts to develop a units strategy and then a counting strategy for solving two-digit addition and subtraction problems. Unifix cubes connected in bars of ten was an effective support for constructing a units strategy. But once such a strategy was developed, it was difficult for some students to construct an alternative, counting strategy, even with supports such as a number line with a special arrow notation. They continued to use the units strategy. Students' initial conception, shaped by the tools they used, had a deep effect on the way they thought about adding and subtracting.

Another example is drawn from work with fourth-grade students and decimal fractions (Hiebert et al. 1991). To understand how different tools may shape students' thinking in different ways, it is helpful to consider the mathematical conceptions that feed into a full understanding of decimal fractions, just as we did earlier for multidigit numbers. Decimal fractions have a dual personality. In some ways they behave like whole numbers. The standard notation conveys the idea that decimal numbers are made up of collections of individual entities grouped by tens. Decimal fractions seem to have an exact and discrete character. But if a quantity is actually measured with decimal units, it becomes clear that the quantity is continuous and that the decimal number is an approximation of the actual amount.

A class of fourth graders studied decimal fractions for several weeks. During about half the time they used tools which appear to highlight the discrete character of decimal fractions, such as base-ten blocks. During the rest of the time they used tools that appear to highlight the continuous character of decimal fractions, such as linear measuring instruments (e.g., meter sticks marked in decimeters and centimeters). Students were interviewed each week; some tasks focused on discrete aspects and some on continuous aspects of decimal fractions. While students were using the discrete tools, their understanding of the discrete aspects of decimals (but not the continuous aspects) improved. While students were using the continuous tools, their understanding of the continuous aspects (but not the discrete aspects) improved. The nature of the tools clearly influenced the way students thought about decimals and the kinds of understandings they developed.

Before concluding this section, we must remind the reader that using tools does not guarantee that they will be used as tools for reflection and thought. Recall the earlier example of adding $\frac{1}{2} + \frac{1}{4}$ and how students, at first, used the tools just as physical answer-getting devices. On the other hand, mathematical tools, such as language, materials, and symbols, *can* be used in ways that influence our thinking. They enable us to solve problems that we would not otherwise solve but, more than that, they shape the way we think about problems. Tools are an integral part of a classroom in which students are constructing important understandings, but all teachers need to think carefully about how tools are being used, and about the relationships between the tools being used and the understandings being developed and appreciate that different tools may support different understandings.

What Is Essential and What Is Optional?

There are many questions regarding the use of mathematical tools for which we do not yet have answers, but there are several points that seem clear: First, tools of some kind are unavoidable and essential for doing mathematics. Second, students develop meaning for tools by actively using them in a variety of situations, to solve a variety of problems. Third, using tools enables students to develop deeper meanings of the mathematics that the tools are being used to examine. This is especially true as students explore relationships between the tools. So, it seems that developing meaning for mathematical tools and for mathematics are all wrapped up together.

What tools should students use? This is where the optional comes in. There does not seem to be a *right* combination of tools for any particular topic. Different tools may support different understandings, and there is no one *correct* understanding. Different students will also construct different understandings from using the same tools because they enter the activity with different conceptions and they may use the tools in somewhat different ways. A particular tool does not guarantee a particular understanding. This means that classrooms in which students are constructing important understandings may differ in the kinds of tools that are in use.

Consider Chapters 7–10 with this mind. There are some interesting differences between classrooms along this dimension.

What seems to be important is not which tool a teacher chooses to introduce into the classroom, but rather that the teacher thinks carefully about the way in which students' thinking might be shaped by using particular tools. This kind of thinking is fruitful because it requires a thoughtful analysis of the mathematics in which students will be engaged and the kinds of understandings that might be left behind. This is just the kind of thinking that enables teachers to plan for the kind of instruction we are describing in these chapters.

6 *Equity and Accessibility*

Equity in learning mathematics and accessibility to learning with understanding is a critical fifth dimension of classrooms.[1] We believe that each student can, and has the right, to learn mathematics with understanding. We also believe that active participation of every student in the mathematical community of the classroom increases the learning opportunities for all. How to design classrooms to ensure equity, especially for traditionally underachieving groups, poses a significant challenge, and there are no simple procedures to follow. However, we offer descriptions of how classrooms can contribute to achieving equity in an attempt to increase the dialog about this critical issue that is facing mathematics education worldwide.

Defining equity has not been easy for anyone and we provide no new definitions (see Fennema 1990 for a discussion). The best that we can do is to offer the beliefs that guided all our deliberations. Every learner—bilingual students, handicapped students, students of all ethnic groups, students who live in poverty, girls, and boys—can learn mathematics with understanding. In order to do this, each student must have access to learning with understanding. We are not proposing that all students will learn the same mathematics to the same degree. We do believe, however, that ensuring that each individual grows in his or her understanding of mathematics will help to eliminate the dramatic differences in learning mathematics which currently exist between advantaged and disadvantaged groups. All classrooms can move toward achieving equity.

Understanding and Equity

Learning with understanding is critical for all children. Some have suggested that *smart* children can invent their own procedures to solve mathematical problems while *slower* children cannot. There are many classrooms where "children from poor families, minority children, and girls receive more instruction on the mastery of basic skills and less instruction on developing conceptual understanding and learning how to apply that conceptual understanding to solve novel problems" (Porter 1991, 130; see also Means and Knapp 1991). We know that all children can learn with understanding. We have seen children categorized as learning disabled—as well as those with much more sophisticated abilities—learn mathematics with understanding. Girls and boys, children of all ability levels, and from all groups have grown in their conceptual understanding of mathematics as they have engaged in problematic situations, reflected about, and discussed their thinking.

Learning with understanding by all children happens when teachers specifically attend to creating a classroom environment that takes into consideration the uniqueness of each individual and attends to critical dimensions of learning characteristics of individuals—not when teachers ignore the traditionally underachieving groups. This means that each child has the opportunity to engage in and reflect on tasks that are mathematically problematic in a social community where his or her thinking is discussed and valued.

Our work with equity has been based on the same assumptions about teaching and learning that has guided all of our work. First, the primary goal of mathematics instruction is the development of conceptual understanding, and progress toward this goal is possible for all students. Second, understanding is developed in the same way for all in the social community of the classroom where students are allowed to engage in problematic tasks, to reflect on their mathematical thinking, and to communicate with others about what they have done. Third, the four dimensions discussed in previous chapters work together to shape a system of instruction that enables all students to learn with understanding.

The Individual and the Group

Notions of equity are built on the belief that each child can and should learn mathematics with understanding. There is a distinct moral imperative embedded in this belief. It is a belief that focuses on an individual's capabilities and rights. However, as important as the individual aspect of equity is, it is not the whole story. The system of instruction that we are describing depends on the participation of all students for its success. Many of the ideas and methods that become objects of group discussion and analysis come from the students, and the classroom depends on each student to provide ideas for discussion. As noted in Chapter 4, the students must share the responsibility for presenting and explaining their solution methods to the class, as well as listening to and understanding others' thinking.

It is important for all students to share in this responsibility because all ideas and methods are potential learning sites. Correct methods are appropriate objects of discussion, as are incorrect methods. A variety of ideas are essential for fueling rich discussions. The likelihood that the class, as a group, will get a variety of ideas on the table for discussion and analysis increases as more students find ways to participate. The group is likely to make the most progress when all students participate and offer ideas and methods for discussion.

Thus, it is not only morally just to create equitable classroom environments: it is also necessary for this system of instruction to work. The mathematics of the classroom must be accessible to all students, and all students must contribute to the learning environment. To the extent that some students are excluded and do not participate, the learning possibilities are diminished for everyone. The academic richness of the classroom depends on full accessibility for all students.

Classrooms That Are Moving Toward Equity

In order to illustrate how our assumptions play out in ongoing classrooms, we provide two examples drawn directly from classrooms. The examples will be presented and discussed in terms of some of the big issues discussed in Chapters 2–5: tasks, communication and reflection within the social culture of the classroom, and the role of the teacher.

Classroom 1

The following took place in a first-grade class in early fall of the school year. The school is located in an economically and ethnically diverse area. The class was taught by Ms. Jenkins, an experienced teacher. The number of students in the class changed often due to the transient nature of the school population. In this episode, the twenty-five students in class were divided into three groups.

One group used counters to find ways to make 10, wrote the number sentence to match, and then told a story (a word problem) to the group to go with the number sentence. Another group sorted attribute blocks and then explained to their group how they had sorted. Another group worked with Ms. Jenkins making the number 30 (the day's date). This discussion began by the children talking about ways to make 30, for example, 5 + 5 + 5 + 5 + 5 + 5. Each child gave at least one way, and after each response the group together checked to see if the response was correct. Next, they solved story problems involving the number 30 that Ms. Jenkins had written using the children's names. A child would read the problem that had his or her name in it, each child in the group would solve the problem, and report individually to the group how she or he had solved it. Ms. Jenkins then asked the children to write story problems about 30 and to write the number sentence that matched each story (Fennema et al. 1993, 566).

Note particularly how children were asked to make connections as they solved problems (e.g., write a number sentence to go with the problem and tell a story that went with it) and how they practiced skills as they worked with the number 30. In this class, the children discussed their thinking in a way that required them to reflect. Not all the children were working at the same level of sophistication, but each child appeared to understand the task he or she was doing. The teacher had designed the tasks so that they were appropriate for children at different levels of understanding. She expected each child to be engaged in problem solving, and the social climate was such that each child's thinking was valued.

Classroom 2

The following episode took place in the spring of the year in a first-grade class. The school serves a stable area of middle-class population, and Ms. Gehn was an experienced teacher. The entire class participated in the same activity.

> Ms. Gehn started the class by saying, "All of our math problems today are going to do with basketball. (The state high school girls' basketball tournament was taking place.) The Badgers (the home team) scored 68 points and their opponents scored 63 points. How many points were scored all together?"

The children each had a set of tools on their desk: slate and chalk, paper and pencil, hundreds-charts, unit counters, and base-ten bars. One child asked the teacher to repeat the problem while most went to work immediately. Each child chose the tool he or she would use. Ms. Gehn wrote the two numbers on the overhead projector and then moved from child to child and observed what each one was doing. She inquired into their thinking ("How did you get that?"), sometimes offered a minor suggestion ("I think you made a mistake counting. Try again."), or modified the problem ("If the Badgers scored 8 points and the opponents scored 13 points, how many were scored altogether?").

After about ten minutes Ms. Gehn had 6 children come individually to the front of the room and demonstrate his or her solution on the overhead projector. Tara directly modeled the solution by putting out 6 ten-bars and 8 unit counters (68); 6 ten-bars and 3 unit counters (63);

counted the tens by 10, (10, 20, 30, . . . 120); and then counted the unit cubes starting at 121, (122, 123, . . . 131). Josh and Ben used two hundreds-charts. Aaron said he just knew that 60 + 60 was 120, 8 + 2 was 10, and one more would be 131 (120 + 10 + 1 = 131). The remaining two children each used a variation of one of the strategies. Other children were expected to listen and to be able to compare their solution strategy to the one being reported.

During the reporting of each of the strategies, Ms. Gehn questioned the children until the solution was clear. She asked questions such as: "Can you tell me what these 6 counters mean? How come you didn't count this pile when you added them up? How did you get 120? What did you think in your head?" (Fennema et al. 1996). Let's consider how the critical features of classrooms play out in each example.

The Role of Tasks

The tasks that learners are asked to do as they learn mathematics must be genuine problems for all learners, and their solutions must provide opportunities for reflection and communication. As suggested in Chapter 2, there are three criteria for selection of tasks: 1) tasks must allow and encourage each student to problematize the mathematics of the situation; 2) tasks must invite each student to use knowledge she or he already possesses; and 3) performance of the task has to leave something of mathematical value behind. The first two of these criteria appear to be critically important when considering issues of equity and accessibility. Too often in the past instructional tasks have not been appropriate for girls and children from diverse cultures because of their lack of experience with the context in which tasks have been set. Furthermore, for some children tasks have been either so easy that they don't become problematic, or so difficult that it is impossible for children to use the knowledge they have.

Consider how each teacher in the examples thought about her children as the context of the tasks were selected. In the first, Ms. Jenkins was working with the day's date, a context that was not ethnically specific to any group in this multicultural classroom. However, it exhibited the core features of tasks which are necessary for children to learn with understanding. It made the mathematics problematic and it connected with where the students were. In the second class, Ms. Gehn selected an event that was taking place in the city in which the school was located. Many have suggested that problems which are embedded in sports events are less appropriate for girls than boys because girls may not understand the context. In this class however, the teacher was able to ascertain that the girls understood the context as well as did the boys. In fact, set in this context, the task provided a real problem for the children that connected with both the boys and the girls.

It should be noted that setting activities in a cultural context for the children in a classroom can either be done by embedding the problems in what is usually thought of as an ethnic culture, or in the everyday culture in which they live. Consider what Ms. Jenkins, an African American who taught an ethnically diverse class, said about her selection of task contexts:

> [I use] situations in the class that students are interested in. I mean, like when we were studying dinosaurs and making up all the different kind of word problems around dinosaurs. Or whenever they discussed an author, finding out how old the author would be today or how old is the book. If the book was written in 1963 and it is 1990, how old is the book today? Is the book older than you? How much older is the book than you? So just making word problems out of anything that comes into the room. Whether it is counting the kids that all have on sneakers one day, or tennis shoes, or if their hair is braided or not braided or whatever. Using the children and using the things that you study, just makes a very, very easy way to form word problems. (Fennema et al. 1993, 560–61)

Although teachers must consider the context of tasks, and it is likely that relevant contexts will more readily engage students' interest, it is important to remember that whether the task is treated as problematic depends as much on the goals students set for themselves as on the task (see Chapter 2). And the goals students set depend largely on the culture of the classroom (see Chapters 3 and 4). It is often the case, as in the classroom examples, that students move quickly beyond the context and engage the mathematics of the situation. What is important is that the contexts of tasks allow all students entry into the situation and allow all students to problematize the situations. The context should not be so limited or unusual for students that it inhibits their ability to understand the situation and its mathematics.

Children in both of the classroom examples were able to engage in a problematic situation at a level which would encourage their learning. Each child was able to problematize the situation, could select tools which were meaningful to him or her, and could invent a procedure to solve the problem.

The Role of Communication and Reflection

While there are many benefits of reflection and communication in classrooms (see Chapters 1–5), one benefit is particularly relevant to moving

toward equity and accessibility. When each child in the classroom participates in the communication process where his/her thinking is valued by
teacher and peers, it communicates to each that he or she is a member of
that community. A person is valued because he or she engages in problematic situations, and reflects about and reports his or her thinking.
Each person also learns to respect and value each other's thinking. The
opportunities and sites for learning increase.

It should be pointed out that communicating one's thinking is not always easy for all students. Children find it difficult to know what is expected, particularly when they have not been asked to communicate
their thinking in previous classrooms. However, like all other skills, reporting on one's thinking can be learned. When sensitive teachers ask
probing questions that help a child to express his or her thinking, or
when children are given the opportunity to hear other children and to
practice the skill of reporting their thinking, they become more willing
and even eager to make sure that everyone understands how they have
handled the task.

There are some issues which have direct relevance to equity and
communication. It has long been known that girls receive less attention
from teachers and actually have fewer opportunities to talk in classrooms
than do boys (AAUW Report 1992). Also, girls may appear to be more
uncomfortable than boys when asked to present their thinking to a large
group, or they may not wish to engage in what may appear to be con-
frontational behavior (such as questioning another child's solution to a
problem). Some children may come to school without the experiences in
discourse that facilitate participation in class discussions. Classroom environments must be created in which these children can learn to communicate and to participate in the social community.

It should be noted that children who are bilingual or for whom English is a second language can, and should, communicate about mathematics as fully as other children. The classrooms described in Chapter 10
shows this is possible. Bilingual children are learning with understanding
by talking and listening to other children.

Just accepting children as they are is insufficient if our goal for mathematics instruction is learning with understanding. Teachers must ensure
that all children learn how to communicate about mathematics. Communication by all children is essential so that they can express their ideas
and reflect on their thinking, so that teachers can understand each child's
thinking, and so that a social community emerges in which all can engage in discussions about mathematics. The learning opportunities for
the entire class increase when all children's ideas can become part of the
discourse.

As in the examples above, classes can be organized so that children can report in a variety of ways. Some children may be more comfortable initially in reporting only to the teacher, or in writing their thinking for others to read. Small group work may provide an environment that is more conducive to reporting for some children. However the class is organized, the critical component is that everyone's thinking is valued when it is shared. When teachers are deeply interested in what each child reports, this interest is demonstrated and soon communicated to all children. It says that thinking is what it means to do mathematics.

It is impossible to prescribe how a classroom should be organized so that an accepting, valuing environment can develop. However, the critical component is the teacher's willingness to spend time and effort in eliciting, understanding, and valuing the thinking of each individual. In the words of a kindergarten teacher:

> I think it is the way the teacher, how should I say it, how she sets the tone of how you're going to share and how we're going to learn from each other so no one is set up, so the kids feel confident or want to share.

The Role of the Teacher

As we said at the beginning of Chapter 3, it is the teacher's responsibility to create a classroom in which all students can engage in problematic tasks, reflect on mathematics and communicate their thoughts and actions. What an awesome responsibility! And what an exhilarating, professional opportunity!

The role of the teacher in classrooms that promote understanding is described in Chapter 3. What is not provided is a prescription that determines day-by-day instructional decisions that teachers must make. Rather, the role of a truly professional teacher is described. This teacher knows each of her or his children well, understands the mathematics that should be learned, selects tasks that enables each student to engage in problematic mathematics, and orchestrates the complex world of the classroom so that children reflect about their thinking and participate in mathematical discussions. The role of the teacher in promoting equity and accessibility involves nothing more than that.

However, as is true with most issues dealing with educational equity, we are confronted with a dilemma: We believe that in an ideal world of learning mathematics, every child should be perceived by his or her teacher as an individual. Decisions about how best to facilitate each child's understanding of mathematics should not be influenced by the child's membership in any group, but rather what she or he knows and can do. In this ideal world, treating children as individuals would lead to equity in mathematics education, and equitable classrooms would not require features beyond those that are critical for any classroom that promotes understanding.

However, this ideal world does not yet exist, and membership in particular groups has led to inequitable treatment of children in mathematics classrooms. We are suggesting that teachers must now be sensitive to membership in these groups in a way that promotes equity rather than inequity. Thus, as one designs equitable classrooms, it is not necessary to identify features other than those we have already described. But equity concerns cannot be ignored or carried out in an incidental manner. Teachers must be especially alert to concerns about equity with traditionally underachieving groups, and they must be doubly concerned that their responsibilities are carried out with each child from each group in the classroom.

This means that the teacher will not treat each student in exactly the same way. The teacher may need to provide different conditions and supports for students with different needs. For example, we noted earlier that some girls may be less comfortable than boys with presenting their problem-solving methods to a large group. The teacher must work out the conditions that allow both girls and boys to feel comfortable communicating about mathematics. In general, teachers must be aware of these kinds of differences that may have promoted inequities in the past and work actively to create learning environments in which each child, regardless of gender, race, ethnicity, and other group memberships, can engage in reflecting on and communicating about mathematics.

We can summarize the point as follows: The general principles of promoting learning with understanding are the same for all groups of learners. However, they have to be interpreted differently as groups differ, and only teachers can make the specific interpretations necessary to ensure that all children learn with understanding.

Conclusions

Although there might be other ways than those we have identified to ensure that all students learn mathematics with understanding, we believe that focusing on developing mathematical understanding by organizing the curriculum around problematic tasks, and engaging all students in reflection and communication is the most promising approach. We also conclude that if, and only if, teachers overtly and consciously consider how classrooms address the problems of equity and accessibility, will there be any possibility of achieving classroom environments in which all students learn with understanding.

We do not provide any easy solutions for the many dilemmas facing teachers and schools as they struggle to achieve equity. However, we have offered some of our insights in the hope that they will enable readers to reflect and communicate about issues dealing with equity and accessibility and thus move toward constructing classrooms that engage each child in learning with understanding.

7 A Day in the Life of One Cognitively Guided Instruction Classroom

Annie Keith teaches a combination first- and second-grade class in an elementary school in Madison, Wisconsin.[1] For the last eight years Ms. Keith has been participating in a program called Cognitively Guided Instruction or CGI (Carpenter and Fennema 1992; Carpenter et al. in press; Fennema et al. 1993; Fennema et al. in press). Cognitively Guided Instruction is not a program of instruction in a traditional sense. There is no curriculum or recommended activities. CGI focuses on teachers' knowledge. The goal is to help teachers better understand children's thinking so that they can help students build on the knowledge that they already have developed. Annie Keith's class provides a glimpse of what is possible when a teacher clearly understands children's thinking and bases her teaching on that understanding.

Ms. Keith's class, which is one of five combination first- and second-grade classes in the school, is made up of ten first graders and ten second graders. Ten of the students are boys, and ten are girls. The school draws from an upper middle-class neighborhood of single homes, several large apartment complexes, and a low-income housing project. Thirteen of the students are European American, four are Hispanic, two are African American, and one is from India. Six of the students receive free or reduced lunch. The students in the class represent a wide range in ability to use basic mathematical concepts and skills. At the beginning of the year, most of the first-grade students had been in a CGI kindergarten and could solve a variety of word problems by modeling the action in the problems using counters or other materials (Carpenter et al. 1993), but most of them had limited knowledge of place value and base-ten number concepts. Several of the first-grade students had more limited counting and modeling skills. In contrast, a number of the second graders understood basic place-value concepts and used more abstract strategies for solving problems.

As we see in the following episode, Ms. Keith deals with this diversity

75

in a number of ways. Children solve problems using a variety different strategies representing different levels of conceptual growth. As a consequence, different children solving the same problem are developing different levels of concepts and skills. If the numbers in a problem represent too great a challenge, children can change them so that the problem is accessible to them. Although a number of problems are solved by the whole class, the children often work at math centers where Ms. Keith can adapt problems for small groups of children. The diversity provides a challenge, but it also provides an opportunity for children to experience a wide variety of strategies. Interactions among children using different strategies provides an opportunity for students to see relations among abstract and more concrete solutions, which provides a basis for them to develop understanding of abstract concepts and procedures.

Word problems provide the basis for almost all instruction in Ms. Keith's class. From the beginning of the year, students have solved a variety of problems using invented modeling and counting strategies. Ms. Keith almost never demonstrates the solution to problems herself, but students spend a great deal of time discussing alternative strategies with Ms. Keith, with other students, and with the whole class.

Little instruction time has been devoted to place-value concepts per se. Students learn place-value concepts as they explore the use of ten blocks and other base-ten materials to solve word problems involving multidigit numbers. From the beginning of the year base-ten blocks, counting frames,[2] and other base-ten materials have been available for students to use to solve problems. Over time, students have become increasingly flexible and efficient in the use of base-ten materials. As their use of the materials has become more automatic, many of them have come to depend less on the manipulations of the physical materials themselves.

Everyday activities like taking the lunch count and sharing snacks are regularly used as contexts for problem-solving tasks. For example, if the box of cookies for today's snack has 6 rows of cookies with 12 cookies in each row, how many cookies are there, and how many cookies can each child have for the snack? Because the treats change each day, this sharing activity provides a variety of problems. Sometimes it is necessary to estimate the number of treats if they are all jumbled together.

Ms. Keith often integrates mathematics with language arts and other subjects. For example, she often uses a story that children are reading or a context from a science or social studies project to construct problems. Children read and write mathematics problems and write about their strategies for solving them in their math journals. Children also engage in extended discussions of mathematical topics that are of interest to them and write essays about mathematics (see one example in Figure 7–1).

7–1 *Mia Forslund's essay about mathematics notebooks*

Mathematics instruction in Ms. Keith's class occurs in a variety of different settings. Students solve problems and engage in discussions about mathematics in small groups and with the entire class. They sometimes work on problems individually and sometimes with other students.

The mathematics lesson for the day often makes use of math centers. During a center cycle every child has the opportunity to work at each center with two or three other students. There usually are five or six centers. At one center students solve word problems that Ms. Keith reads to them. Working with three or four students allows Ms. Keith to focus on a few students and interact with them about their strategies as they are solving problems. She can adapt problems to individual students and provide appropriate support when they need it. These interactions provide Ms. Keith an opportunity to assess the strategies each child is using and follow up with questions and problems that might encourage a child to adopt a more advanced strategy if Ms. Keith thinks the child is ready.

Another group of students usually writes word problems to share with the rest of the class. Following center time, several students from this group generally read their problems to the whole class for the other students to solve. During this sharing time, the student-author takes on the role of the teacher, asking questions and calling on students to share their strategies.

Other center activities focus on topics like geometry, graphing, and reasoning. There generally is one center at which students play a mathematics game. The objective for this center is not only to learn mathematics by playing these games but also to develop some appreciation for how rules for games are structured. Near the end of the year, students in this center construct their own games, using reasoning and logic to decide on appropriate rules.

At another center, students might be involved in a variety of activities involving some sort of geometric constructions or representing data with graphs. The activities at this center generally have a clear objective. At another center students are provided opportunity for relatively unstructured exploration with math tools that might be used in more structured ways at other times. In this center students make patterns or build some sort of structure using geoboards, tangrams, pattern blocks, Legos™, and the like. They construct the pattern or building and then draw a picture of it. These activities provide an opportunity for students to represent patterns and two- and three-dimensional shapes.

Thus, there is variety in the kinds of mathematical problems and issues that students deal with and a variety of contexts in which they deal with them. The constant is that students are always challenged to think and to try to make sense of what they are doing. They are challenged to take responsibility for monitoring their own learning and understanding.

But learning is not an isolated individual activity; the students share ideas with one another, and they learn from one another and learn to respect each other's ideas.

It is difficult, if not impossible, to provide a complete perspective of any classroom, much less a classroom as complex as Ms. Keith's. We have chosen to focus on a single day and to let Ms. Keith's words and the students' words tell as much of the story as possible.[3] It would be inaccurate to say that this is a typical day; there is too much variety to characterize any day as typical. But the interactions that take place on this day are characteristic of interactions that are seen on any day in this class.

A Day in the Life

On this day in late March, the students engage in a whole class activity rather than going to centers. A colleague of Ms. Keith's has sent several problems to individual students in the class, and these problems are shared with the whole class. The math period extends from opening activities to morning recess, a period of about an hour and a half. In this time the students solve and discuss two problems.

Opening Activities

The students are sitting in a circle on a rug in one corner of the room. They have no paper, pencil, or other math tools. The day begins with the lunch count. Today 6 students are taking hot lunch and 10 students are taking cold lunch. Ms. Keith turns that into a problem.

Ms. Keith: How many kids is that?

Students: Sixteen.

Ms. Keith: How do you know? Jamie, how do you know?

Jamie: When you add something to a 10 or 20, like anything under 10, it'll make like 9 to 10, it'll make 19.

Ms. Keith: OK. Randy?

Randy: Ten and 5 is 15, cause on number munchers we do multiples. Fifteen is a multiple of 5, and 1 more is 16.

Ms. Keith: Anna, would you do it?

Anna: Ten, 11, 12, 13, 14, 15, 16.

Ms. Keith: Good. So you counted up? Kim?

Kim: I did it like Anna.

Ms. Keith: OK. How many kids do we have gone today?

If everyone is present there are twenty students in the class, and the students quickly respond that four students are absent. Again, a number of students are given opportunity to explain their strategies for finding the answer.

Math Problems for the Day

Next Ms. Keith announces that she has two problems from Ellen in Pittsburgh. Ellen is a university teacher who spent a lot of time in Ms. Keith's class the preceding year, so all the second graders who were in Ms. Keith's class last year know her. She has corresponded with the class by e-mail throughout the year, and she often sends problems to individual students. Today the whole class works on problems that Ellen sent to two students.

Ms. KEITH: I have two problems from Ellen in Pittsburgh. Carla, I took your problem. I thought Ellen would like to see how everyone did it. I also took a problem for Sam. I put each problem on a sheet of paper. I want you to figure out two ways and write them down on the paper. We will come back and explain how we did it. It will help if you write down exactly how you did it.

Here's the first problem. Sam found 123 fossils. He found 456 more, but he lost 98. How many fossils does he have left?

If the numbers are too big, what should you do?

STUDENTS: Change them.

Ms. KEITH: Should you change them to be really easy numbers or numbers that are challenging for you?

STUDENTS: Numbers that are challenging.

Ms. KEITH: Here's Carla's problem. Carla drew 18 pictures on Steve's cast. Dan drew 23 pictures, and Ms. Keith drew 37 pictures on Steve's cast. How many pictures did they all draw on Steve's cast?

Solving the Problems

Ms. Keith gives each student a sheet of paper with both problems written on it and room to record their strategies for solving them. The students disperse to different parts of the room to solve the problems. They use a variety of math tools. Some students use counting frames, some use base-ten blocks, and some use paper and pencil. A number of students work alone, and some work in small groups of two or three students. Some students who are working alone periodically find another student to compare answers and strategies. Students record their solutions on the paper using a variety of representations. Some students make tally marks to solve the problem or to show how they used individual counters. Others draw pictures of base-ten blocks. Others use tree diagrams or arrow diagrams to solve the problem or to record their strategy (see Figures 7–3, 7–4, 7–6, and 7–7 for examples of tree diagrams and Vicki's discussion at the end of the day for an example of an arrow diagram).

Ms. Keith talks to individual students about their solutions. Rather than moving quickly from student to student, she spends a great deal of time listening to each student explain his or her strategies. She does not cut the student off when she understands how the student has solved the problem; rather she lets the student provide a complete explanation of the strategy used to solve the problem. The whole time the student is explaining the problem, Ms. Keith listens intently. In so doing she models the listening skills that she expects the students to develop and communicates to them that their strategies are important.

The following is an exchange between Ms. Keith and Karen about how Karen solved the problem about the pictures on Steve's cast. Karen has solved the problem in several ways, and has gotten different answers. Ms. Keith works through her solutions with her, both to look for the error and to give Karen the opportunity to explain her strategies.

KAREN: I got two different answers. On this one I got 70, and on this one I got 78.

Ms. KEITH: Show me this one (*pointing to the solution in which Karen got 70*).

KAREN: Eighteen and 23 is 41.

Ms. KEITH: How do you know that?

KAREN: I used the cubes (*referring to the base-ten blocks*).

Ms. KEITH: Can you show me what you did?

Karen puts out 1 ten block and 8 ones blocks. She then puts out 2 tens blocks and 3 ones (see Figure 7–2). She counts the tens blocks and then continues counting the individual ones blocks "30, 31, 32, 33, . . . 41."

Ms. KEITH: So, is there a bug there?[4]

KAREN: No.

Ms. KEITH: So, now what are you going to do?

Karen puts 3 more tens and 7 ones with the ten blocks representing 41. She counts the tens "10, 20, 30, 40, 50, 60." She then counts 10 ones and trades them for a ten bar. She continues counting "70, 71, 72, 73, . . . 78."

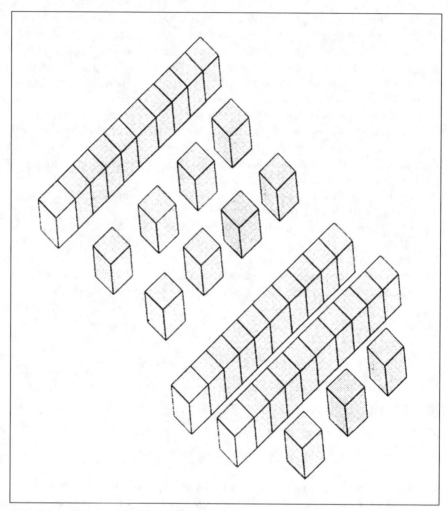

7–2 Karen's base-ten block representation of 18 + 23

KAREN: This time I got 78.

MS. KEITH: Why do you think that this time you got 78?

KAREN: Maybe I forgot the 7 and the 1 and just brought down the tens. *(She appears to be referring to the 7 from the 37 and the 1 left over from combining 8 and 3 to make another ten.)*

MS. KEITH: So now what are you going to do?

KAREN: Do it again.

Karen then explains another solution in which she also used the tens blocks but first combined 18 and 37. Then she explains a third solution that involves much more abstract reasoning. Her representation of this solution appears in Figure 7–3.

KAREN: Then on this last one, I added the 20 and the 3.

MS. KEITH: The 20 and the 3?

KAREN: I mean the 20 and the 30. That made 50. I knew that 2 and 3 is 5, so 20 and 30 is 50. Then I added the 7 and the 3. That made 10; and 10 and the 50 that made 60; and adding the 10 from the 18, that made 70; and I added the 8 that made 78.

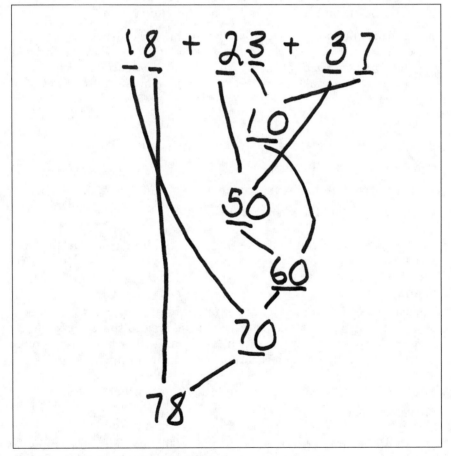

7–3 Karen's solution for 18 + 23 + 37

Ms. KEITH: Excellent! Do you want to try this one now *(indicating the other problem)*?

While Ms. Keith is talking to Karen, the other students are working individually or in small groups. Three students have found that they have different answers. They check their answers with a calculator and then go back to work to try to find their errors.

Two other students discuss the second problem. Vicki tells Roger that she has two different answers for the problem about Sam's fossils. The correct answer is 481, but neither child knows that yet.

VICKI: On this one *(indicating a tree diagram that she has used to represent her solution)* I got 496. On this one *(indicating the tree diagram in Figure 7–4)* I got 472. I can't seem to find what I did wrong.

ROGER: This one looks like it would be the one, because it looks like the easier way. *(Roger studies the tree diagram in Figure 7–4 for several minutes. From his remarks it appears that he is working backward from the answer.)* What's 8 take away 9; I mean 9 take away 8 *(referring to A on Figure 7–4)*?

VICKI: One.

Roger: I know, but that made it a 2. *(Vicki changes the 2 to a 1.)*

ROGER: And what's 90 minus—

VICKI: No! Five hundred seventy take way 90, and I got 480.

ROGER: It says 470 here *(B on Figure 7–4)*.

The discussion continues, as the two children continue to check Vicki's solution.

Sharing

After the class has worked for about forty minutes on the two problems, Ms. Keith calls the students back to the rug area to share the strategies they used to solve the problems. She starts out with a short discussion of the rules for sharing, which is part of the sharing routine.

Ms. KEITH: How are you going to understand each other's ways?

STUDENTS: Listen!

All of the students reread aloud the problem about the pictures on Dan's cast, and Ms. Keith calls on Diana to share first.

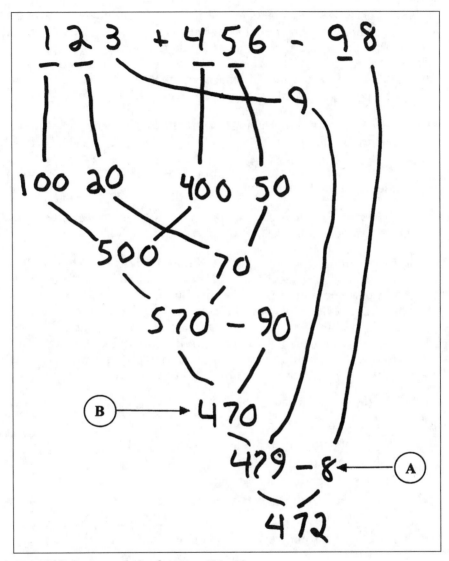

7–4 Vicki's incorrect solution for 123 + 456 – 98

DIANA: I put 18 tally marks.

MS. KEITH: Can you show us?

DIANA: *(Draws tally marks on the board and explains as she does it.)* I put 18, then 23. *(Long pause as she draws tally marks.)* Then I put 37 *(draws 37 tally marks)*. Then I counted them all up.

Diana draws 18 tally marks in one row. She then draws a row of 20 tally marks and 3 tally marks in a row just below it. She then draws 30 tally marks in the same row as the 3 tally marks, leaving some space between the two groups of tally marks. She draws 7 tally marks below the 30. She then counts all the tally marks by one, but the tally marks are close together, and she makes a counting error.

DIANA: Seventy-nine? But I got 78 first. I think I messed up counting these *(points to the group of 37).*

Diana tries to recount the 37 tallies, but gets mixed up and starts over several times. Karen comes up to help her.

KAREN: You weren't supposed to count this one *(points to one of the 3 tally marks from the 23),* because it was part of the 23.

Diana recounts each of the sets and then recounts the whole collection again. The whole class listens and watches patiently as Diana counts the sets over several times. This time she gets 80. Because the tally marks are small and close together, it is difficult for the students or Ms. Keith to pick out when Diana has missed a tally mark or counted one twice. Ms. Keith does not count the tally marks herself or ask one of the other students to do so. That would be taking Diana's solution away from her. The class might help her, but this is Diana's problem to work out.

MS. KEITH: What's hard about doing it with all those tally marks?

SUSAN: They are small and you might count one twice.

AARON: You could cross them out as you count.

BETH: Another way would be to get an abacus. It would be easier with something bigger than those tallies.

MS. KEITH: Do you want to try it with something else and then come back?

DIANA: Yes.

MS. KEITH: OK. Pick someone else who did it a different way. *(Diana picks Karen, who has her hand up indicating that she has a different solution. Then Diana goes off to work on the problem.)*

KAREN: *(Presents her third solution. She draws her tree diagram [Figure 7–3] on the board and provides the following explanation as she draws it.)* First I added the 20 from the 23 and the 30 from the 37, and that made 50. Because I know that 2 and 3 is 5, so 20 and 30 will be 50. Then I added the 7 and the 3 together. That made 10. I added the 10 and the 50, and that made 60. And then I added the 10 from the 18; that made 70. Then I added the 8 with the 70. That made 78.

Ms. KEITH: Any questions for Karen? *(Pause as she waits for questions)* Karen, will you pick someone please. *(Karen calls on Rick.)*

RICK: *(Brings a counting frame to explain his strategy [Figure 7–5].)* First I counted out 18. I knew that this was 10.

Rick moves over the whole top row and then counts 8 in the second row. He is having a hard time holding the counting frame and moving the beads, and the beads that he has moved slide back and forth.

Ms. KEITH: Maybe if you put it on the chalk tray, that would be easier.

RICK: *(Moves the counting frame to the chalk tray and counts out 18 beads again. He continues, counting out 23 and 37 in the same way [Figure 7–5a].)* But I knew that here's 3 and here's 3 *(pointing to the 3 from the 23 and the 3 that was left over from making the 7 in 37 [see B and C in Figure 7–5a]).* So I knew that I could put this one over here *(he slides over the 7 beads on the same row as the 3 in the 23, making another ten)* and take back these *(pushes back the 7 from the 37 [See Figure 7–5b]).* That would still be the same thing.

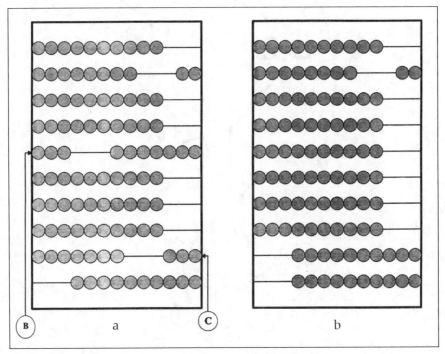

7–5 Rick's solution for 18 + 23 + 37, using a counting frame

Rick then counts the beads, counting the tens "10, 20, 30, 40, 50, 60, 70." He then starts to count on the remaining 8 beads but stops, realizing that he does not actually have to count the 8 remaining beads.

RICK: Seventy-one, 72. Wait, 78. Because this was 18, so it would be 8, so I wouldn't have to count up.

MS. KEITH: Any questions for Rick? *(Pause)* Are all these ways different? *(Students respond, "Yes.")* Are they all good ways? *("Yes.")* Would you call on someone, Rick? *(Rick calls on James.)*

JAMES: I know this one makes 30 *(connects 10 from the 18 and the 20 from the 23 [see Figure 7–6])*. I know 3 and 7 makes 10. Thirty and 30, that makes 60. Ten and 60, that makes 70. Eight and 70, that makes 78.

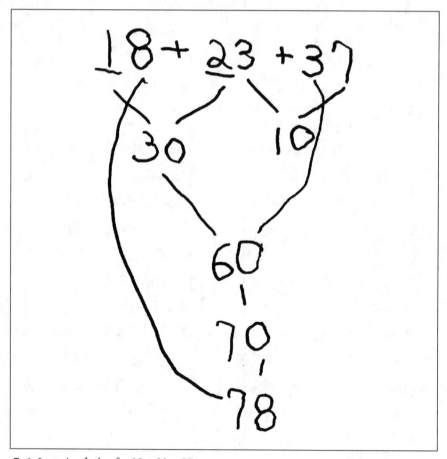

7–6 *James's solution for 18 + 23 + 37*

MS. KEITH: Is James's way similar to any other way?

WES: Similar to Karen's.

MS. KEITH: So what's similar?

WES: He pulled down the tens, and they both had 60.

MS. KEITH: How are they different?

CARLA: Karen didn't use the 20 from the 23 and the 10 from the 18 first. She used the 20 from the 23 and the 30 from the 37.

MS. KEITH: So does it matter what number you start with or which you put together?

STUDENTS: No.

Another student shares a strategy similar to Karen's with a slight variation in it. When she is done Diana has returned, and Ms. Keith gives her the opportunity to share her new solution. This time Diana has used the counting frame. She makes 18 by first moving the top row of 10 over without counting and then counting out 8 beads in the second row. She is holding the counting frame, and has the same problem Rick did with the beads sliding. She also gets her hair stuck in the counting frame. Ms. Keith untangles her hair and volunteers to hold the counting frame. Diana makes the 18 again, and then makes 23 counting each bead by one. She then makes the 37 by moving 3 tens and then counting 7 ones. To solve the problem she counts the tens by ten ("10, 20, 30, 40, 50, 60") and then counts all the rest by ones ("61, 62, 63, . . . 78"). Thus, in solving the problem, Diana sometimes uses her emerging knowledge of tens to help her count, and sometimes she does not.

Ms. Keith asks her if that was easier than using the tally marks. Diana says, "Yes." When Ms. Keith asks her why, Diana responds that they were bigger. She does not mention that the counting frame helped her to use tens to count and keep track, but Ms. Keith does not push that issue at this time. The class moves on to the next problem. Vicki is the first child to share. She constructs the tree diagram in Figure 7–7 as she describes how she solved the problem.

VICKI: First I took the 100 off the 123. Then I took the 20 off the 123. Then I took the 400 off the 456. Then I took the 50 off the 456. Then I added the 400 and the 100, and I know that would be 500, because I know 4 plus 1 is 5. With hundreds it would be 500. Then I added the 20 and the 50; that makes 70. Then I added 500 and 70; that's 570. Then I took away 90. I knew that 20 plus 70 made 90. So I took the 70 off the 570. Then I took 20 away from 500. That made 480.

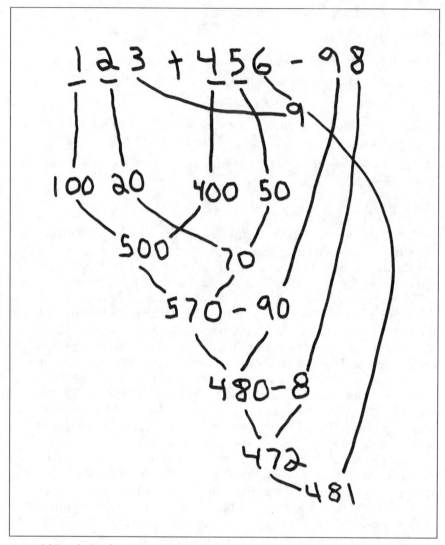

7-7 *Vicki's solution for 123 + 456 − 98*

Then I took 8 away. That made 472. Then I added 6 and 3. That made 9. Then I added that to 472. That made 481. That's what I got.

After asking if there are any questions for Vicki, Ms. Keith says that she saw her solve it another way using an arrow diagram. Vicki says that is her third way, but she is not finished. Ms. Keith asks if she would like to finish it and come back to share it with the class.

The next child to share a solution is Sarah. She has changed the first two numbers, so her problem is 100 + 202 − 98.

SARAH: First I took 100 and then 202 *(first she puts out a one hundred flat and then 2 more hundred flats and 2 ones)*. Then I wanted to take away 98, so I got one of these *(picks up a ten bar)* to mark 90, and one of these *(a one cube)* to mark 8. *(She puts the ten bar on one of the hundred flats so that one row of ten is above the ten bar [see Figure 7–8].)* I knew that would be 90, because 10 less than 100 is 90. Then I counted up *(she counts along the single uncovered row, and puts the one cube to mark the 8).* And I counted all the rest and I got 294. *(On the covered hundred flat she should only count the remaining 2. Instead she counts the 90 and the 2. In other words, rather than subtracting 98, she has only subtracted 8.)*

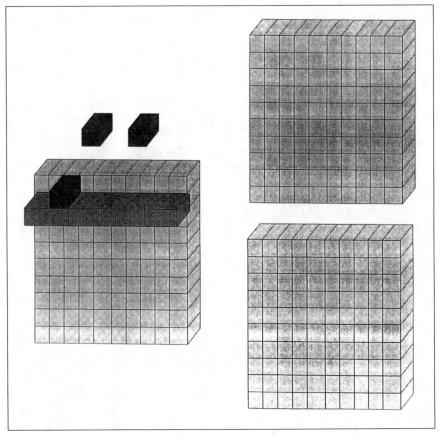

7–8 Sarah's solution for 100 + 202 − 98

Ms. KEITH: When you counted what did you do? Will you show us how you counted?

KAREN: *(Observes that Sarah is not subtracting the 90)* You're not supposed to count the 90. You're only supposed to count these *(points to the 2 squares at the end).*

Before the issue can be resolved, it is time for recess. Before she goes out to recess, Vicki wants to share her solution using the arrow diagram with Ms. Keith. She gives the following explanation as she writes on the board:

$$100 + 400 \rightarrow 500 + 23 \rightarrow 523 + 56 \rightarrow 579 - 8 \rightarrow 571 - 90 = 481$$

VICKI: I took the 100 out of the 123 and added it to the 400 out of the 456. That made 500 plus 23 off the 123 made 523, and the 56 from 456 made 579.

Ms. KEITH: How did you know that? How did you know 523 plus 56 equaled 579?

VICKI: Well, I knew 6 plus 3 is 9, and 20 plus 5 is 70.

Ms. KEITH: Twenty plus 5 is 70?

VICKI: Wait, 20 plus 50 is 70. Then I added 79 to 500. That made 579. Then I took away 8, and because 9 was the one at the end in the 579, I knew that there would be 1 left in the ones after I took away the 8. Then minus 90. Well, I knew 20 plus 70 was 90. I took away 70 from 571; that made 501, and I took away 20. That made 581; I mean 481.

This is the first time that Ms. Keith has seen Vicki break up numbers to subtract like she did in subtracting 90 from 571, and Ms. Keith would like her to reflect on the strategy so that she can use it again in the future. Ms. Keith asks Vicki another question to see if she will do it again and can articulate what she has done.

Ms. KEITH: Can I ask you another question? What if the numbers were 576 minus 39?

VICKI: 576 minus 30 make 546. Let's see minus 9, makes 530 *(writes 53 then there is a pause as she tries to figure out what goes in the ones' place).* Let's see, 6 minus, um 546 minus 9, um 537 *(writes the 7 to complete the 537).*

Ms. KEITH: Why?

VICKI: Because I know . . . 7 + 3 makes 40, and then if you add that 3 to 6 that makes 9. So 537.

Vicki's explanation is a little unclear, but she appears to be working backward from the answer 537. She essentially is saying that if you add 9 to 537 you get 546, so 546 − 9 = 537. To do the calculation, she breaks the addition down, first adding 3 to 37 and then adding 6 to the result. She is using combinations of numbers, but in a different way than she did in subtracting 571 − 90. Ms. Keith probes further to see if Vicki can think about the problem as she did before.

Ms. Keith: Are you sure?

Vicki: Sure.

Ms. Keith: *(Moves over to the original problem which involved subtracting 571 − 90.)* You know over here you said that you thought about combinations. You said that when you were subtracting the 90. . . I know that 70 and 20 makes 90 so I can take the 70 off here, and then I still have to subtract 20 more. Can you do that with the ones here *(pointing to the new problem, 576 − 39)*? Do you think about that?

Vicki: It would work. I know that 6 + 3 is 9, so I took the 6 out, and it's down to 40, 540. I take 3 away 40 − 3 is 7, 37. That's just like the 571 minus 90.

Vicki joins the other children at recess. After recess Sarah is given a chance to resolve her solution. She understands that her goal is to take away 98, but she has gotten mixed up in the procedure of doing that. The students decide that it would be easier to cover up the 90 with another hundred flat to avoid the confusion of what has been taken away. After several false starts, Sarah solves the problem correctly and winds up with the answer of 204. When she is done Rick offers another way of subtracting.

Rick: It's not really covering them up. You could take 2 and put them right here *(puts 2 unit cubes on the corner of one of the hundred flats)* and count the uncovered ones . . . because 2 and 98 equal 100. *(When Rick refers to counting the uncovered ones, he intends to subtract the uncovered squares. He actually means that he would count the 2 covered ones in calculating the final answer.)*

It is time for reading.

Discussion

In this episode we see students engaged in challenging tasks. Although a major part of the lesson involves learning to add and subtract two- and three-digit numbers, the students are not learning a routine skill. Not only are the tasks set in story problem contexts, the construction of strategies for adding and subtracting two- and three-digit numbers is taken as a problem-solving activity. Although there is a wide range in the level of understanding of basic place value concepts, all of the students are able to solve the problems in ways that make sense to them.

The students also do not consider the tasks routine in the sense of being boring. They find the problems challenging and interesting. On this day they stay engaged in solving two problems for over forty minutes, and they listen and discuss alternative strategies for another half hour. One reason that the students are engaged is that the tasks make sense to them, and they have control of how they solve them. If a problem is too difficult, they can change it. If a strategy does not make sense, the students can use a more concrete strategy. If a strategy starts to become routine and boring, they can try an alternative more challenging strategy. Above all, the students find the problems engaging because they solve them in ways that make sense to them, in ways that they understand.

Learning with Understanding

It is useful to return to our characterization of understanding in Chapter 1 to consider how Ms. Keith's instruction supports learning with understanding. Understanding is characterized in terms of how knowledge is connected. Ms. Keith's instruction offers a variety of opportunities for students to connect emerging concepts and strategies to concepts and strategies that already make sense to them. Students start out building on modeling strategies that they naturally use to solve problems. More advanced and abstract strategies build on these basic strategies. The interactions with Diana and Karen show two students on the verge of developing more advanced strategies. Diana starts out describing a strategy that uses individual tallies, and makes minimal use of base-ten concepts. But her initial strategy shows some emerging understanding of ten, as she separates the tallies representing 20 from the those representing the 3 ones and the 30 tallies from the 7. When she uses the counting frame, the ten structured organization of the counters on the frame facilitates her use of tens in her solution. She is still quite tentative in her use of tens, but she appears to see how this strategy relates to her previous strategy.

Karen starts out modeling with tens blocks. In her final solution she combines tens and ones without the blocks. From this one observation it is not clear whether she could have come up with the third solution without first solving the problem with the blocks, but by the time she shares, she is able to describe the strategy without using or even referring to the blocks. The invented algorithms used by a number of students in Ms. Keith's class are essentially abstractions of the blocks procedures. By reflecting on the blocks procedures and talking about them, students become aware of the actions on the blocks and can think about these actions at an abstract level, combining the tens, combining the ones, and so on. The manipulations of the blocks become objects of reflection. At some point the numbers involved in counting the blocks also become objects of reflection so that the students can operate on the numbers without having to manipulate the blocks. Karen appears to be going through this transition.

A Classroom Culture That Supports the Development of Understanding

A key feature of Ms. Keith's class that contributes to the development of understanding is the continuing discussion of alternative strategies. The students in Ms. Keith's class regularly are called upon to articulate their solutions, to describe in words what they have done with the blocks. In order to be able to describe their strategies, they need to reflect upon them, and to decide how to report them verbally. Initially the descriptions are of procedures that have already been carried out. Eventually the words that students use to describe their manipulations of tens materials become the solutions themselves. Thus, the verbal description of modeling strategies provides a basis for connecting manipulations of tens materials and invented algorithms using numbers only.

The discussion of alternative strategies also contributes to the development of understanding in other ways than encouraging students to reflect upon and articulate their solution processes. Because a number of different strategies for solving a given problem are discussed, different strategies and representations are continuously juxtaposed. This offers the potential for relating different strategies and representations on a regular basis, as we saw in the discussions of similarities and differences between Karen's and James's strategies and in the presentation of Vicki's two different solutions.

With the continual sharing, students learn from other students, and this would seem to offer the potential for students to attempt to imitate strategies that they do not understand. That occurs very infrequently in Ms. Keith's class. None of the students describe strategies that they do not understand on the day depicted above. The discussion of alternative strategies encourages students to use strategies that they understand. They know that they have to be able to describe whatever strategy they use, so they are not inclined to use a strategy that they cannot explain.

Mathematical Tools for Supporting Understanding

The students in the class use a variety of tools to solve problems, and the tools used afford a variety of different solutions. The two different solutions that Diana shares with the class illustrate how tools help shape the way the children think about numbers and problems. In Diana's initial solution with tally marks, she demonstrates limited use of tens and does not use groups of tens to solve the problem. The fact that beads are arranged in rows of ten on the counting frame provides support for Diana to use groups of tens in her second solution. In a similar way the tree diagrams and the arrow diagrams provide support for other students to think about their abstract solutions. The calculations involve a number of steps, and the diagrams provide a way of identifying and keeping track of the partial sums.

These tools not only provide support for children's thinking as they solve problems, they serve as a basis for communication about the strategies. When children present their strategies to the class, the tools provide a basis for discussing alternative strategies and identifying potential errors. For example, the children can see the potential difficulties that Diana is having counting the tally marks, and they can remember differences between strategies presented using tree diagrams because the diagrams provide graphic records that clearly communicate the sequence of steps in the solutions. In the discussion between Vicki and Roger, we see how the tree diagram provides a record of Vicki's solution that Roger can analyze and talk about with Vicki. The notation serves as a basis for communication between the two children so that they can talk about specific steps in Vicki's solution. In the same way, the arrow diagrams provide a basis for Ms. Keith to discuss with Vicki specific aspects of her solutions.

Ms. Keith introduces the various learning supports as tools for solving and communicating about problems, and the children have the latitude to use them in ways that make sense to them and are useful to them to solve problems. For example, the base-ten blocks and the counting frame are available to solve problems from the beginning of the year, before there is any discussion of place value. Initially, most children count each of the single beads in the counting frame or the small blocks making up a ten block. Over time, they start to count the collections of ten, and they become increasingly efficient in working with groups of ten. Diana's and Rick's solutions illustrate this progression.

Ms. Keith introduces the tree and arrow diagrams as notations for recording solutions. She does not make a big deal of teaching the children to use the notations; she simply starts using them to record children's solutions on the board as they are sharing them with the class. These notations provide a record of the solution that the class can use to talk about the different solutions. These notations provide efficient ways to record solutions, and the children begin to adopt them to record their own solutions in their math journals. As the problems get more difficult, the notations become more than records of the ways that the children solve the problems: They become tools for thinking.

Equity

We have proposed that equity entails the active participation of all students in the class. Not all students will exhibit the same level of abstract thinking, but all students are part of the learning community and their thinking is valued and treated with respect by the teacher and other students. The students in Ms. Keith's class clearly value and respect all the strategies of every student. Even though many students no longer need to use materials to solve problems, they all attend while Diana explains her very basic strategy, and they actively participate in helping her locate her errors and choose tools that may be less prone to miscounting.

One reason that the children in Ms. Keith's class value every child's strategies is that they see how the strategies are interrelated, and that the basic strategies are valid strategies too. In other words, the focus on understanding supports a commitment to equity while at the same time a commitment to equity on the part of Ms. Keith and the students contributes to the understanding of all students in the class.

The following example from the prior year's class further illustrates how all students are treated with respect and integrated into the learning community. The episode, which is excerpted from Ansell (1995), takes place following small group work at the learning centers. As part of the regular routine, students who had worked at the story writing center share their word problems with the class. During this time the student-author takes on the role of the teacher, asking questions and calling on students to share their strategies. One of the students sharing this day was Rachel, a girl with Down's Syndrome. She sat in the rocker—which was usually reserved for Ms. Keith—and read her problem. The students quietly listened to her read the problem:

> I love spaghetti! Yesterday I ate 5 spaghetti dinners. Today I ate 3 more spaghetti dinners. How many spaghetti dinners did I eat?

Rachel watched with a smile as students responded with the same enthusiasm they displayed in response to [more difficult problems]. Students could be seen using their fingers alone or in combination with others', putting together counters, and writing strategies in their notebooks. After a couple of minutes Rachel called on students to share. [As with more complex problems] their strategies were at a variety of levels of sophistication.

With the exception of the author, this problem was a relatively easy problem for all the students to solve. Furthermore, it used a number fact that many knew on a recall level. However, when the problem was read, children did not immediately raise their hands with the answer, and although I knew that four of the first five students called on to share knew by recall that 5 and 3 was 8, to my surprise (and Ms. Keith's), the first five students verbalized strategies other than recall. . . .

Immediately after Rachel read the problem, one student had called out "that's easy!" This student, a relatively new member of the class, was quickly reprimanded by another who responded that it was not easy for the problem's author. Neither the new student nor his scolder gave recall as their solution strategy, but when Ms. Keith asked, both indicated that they did just know it. After class I asked these students and two others who similarly had recall knowledge but shared another strategy why they chose to share the strategy they had. The child who reprimanded the new student said it was important for him to make sure the author understood how he knew it. (Ansell 1995, 2–5)

The Role of the Teacher

The ways that Ms. Keith interacts with her students during the day described in this chapter say a great deal about her perception of her role as a teacher. But rather than reviewing this day, we would like to discuss several additional examples from her class that provide an even sharper perspective of her perception of her role in the classroom. A number of students in the class are intrigued by numbers, and they raise hypotheses about them. During the course of the year the class has engaged in recurring discussions of large numbers, negative numbers, and even and odd numbers. Ms. Keith lets the students engage in discussion and challenge each other's ideas. Although she may try to clarify what a given student has said, she refrains from becoming the source of knowledge or the arbitrator of what is right and what is wrong.

Although the students learn about properties of negative numbers, odd and even numbers, and the like in these discussions, Ms. Keith has a more far-reaching goal. The students are learning about the nature of logical argument and what it takes to justify a hypothesis. For example, one student initiated a discussion one day saying that he had a theory about even and odd numbers. Even and odd numbers had been discussed in class on a number of previous occasions, but many students' understanding of them was still quite tenuous. This student said that if you add two even numbers you will always get an even number, and if you add an even and an odd number you will get an odd number. Several examples were put on the board to illustrate this hypothesis. Many students appeared to accept the proposition and thought that the examples supported it. One student, however, challenged the evidence. He said that just because it worked for those numbers did not mean that it would work for all even and odd numbers. The discussion continued with other students providing other arguments for the proposition. As often is the case in these discussions, the issue was not resolved, and Ms. Keith did not step in to try and get closure on whether the proposition was valid or not. Instead she invited the students to go off and think about it some more, to try some other examples and see what they could figure out.

Ms. Keith works hard to encourage students to try to resolve issues among themselves rather than turning to her for authority. She even refuses to be the source of authority when students are discussing issues that depend on accepted convention and cannot be resolved through logic alone. For example, for several weeks the class engaged in an ongoing debate of what a million was. Some students argued that a million came after a thousand. (By this they meant that 10,000 was a million, not that a million was the next number in the counting sequence after 1000.) Other students argued that 1,000,000 was a million. There is no way to resolve this difference through logic: It is a matter of convention. But Ms. Keith believes that there are other sources for finding this kind of knowledge, and she does not want the students to regard her role as *the* source of knowledge. Although it might be suggested that such a discussion is a waste of time because the question of what number the word a million stands for cannot be resolved through discussion, Ms. Keith's goal was not just learning factual knowledge about a million. The debate provided a context in which students interacted with the issue of what kinds of knowledge can be resolved by logical argument and what kinds depend on authority or convention. In the process of the discussion, interesting arguments were posed. One child proposed that 10,000 cannot be a million because it is ten thousand. Another student countered that 1,600 is one thousand six hundred and is also sixteen hundred, so numbers can have more than one name.

A Community of Learners

The class is a true community of learners in which Ms. Keith participates along with her students. She expects students to listen to one another, and she listens to them and clearly communicates that she respects what they have to say. Ms. Keith's role in the class is summed nicely up in the following excerpt from a discussion on the importance of listening:

Ms. KEITH: Is it important for me to listen?

STUDENTS: Yes?

Ms. KEITH: Why?

JAMES: You're the teacher.

Ms. KEITH: So?

ANNA: You want to understand what we know.

Ms. KEITH: Is it important for me to know?

VICKI: Yes. Because if you don't know what we already know, you'll teach us, and we already know it.

Ms. KEITH: Why else is it important for me to listen?

KAREN: Because you might learn things that you don't know.

Ms. KEITH: That's right, I learn a lot from kids.

That comment goes a long way toward explaining what makes Ms. Keith's classroom a place for learning with understanding both for her and for the students.

8 A Day in the Life of a Conceptually Based Instruction Classroom

The classroom described in this chapter was part of the Conceptually Based Instruction (CBI) project directed by James Hiebert and Diana Wearne of the University of Delaware.[1] The project provided children in grades 1–3 with instruction on the topics of place value and multidigit addition and subtraction that was an alternative to conventional textbook instruction. Additional information about this project may be found in Hiebert and Wearne (1993, 1992).

The rationale that guided the design of the alternative instruction is consistent with the definition of understanding proposed in Chapter 1: understanding is built through establishing relationships. Three kinds of relationships are emphasized: relationships between what one already knows and new information, relationships among different ways of representing information, and relationships among different methods of solving similar problems.

The alternative instruction supports students' efforts to connect new experiences with existing knowledge by presenting tasks that often require modifying previous methods or building new methods from those students already understand. Familiar tools are always available to develop new methods and help to link the old with the new.

The alternative instruction also emphasizes the different ways that numbers can be represented (with written numerals, oral language, and physical materials) and the connections that can be established among these forms. Class discussions focus on how different representations can be used and how they are similar and different.

Finally, students are expected to develop and use methods for solving problems that they understand. As they share and explain their methods and listen to those of others, they are asked to build connections by considering how the methods are alike and different, and what advantages different methods afford.

The three ways of building relationships (connecting new with familiar,

101

comparing different forms of representation, and comparing solution methods) are supported during instruction through an integrated process that begins with situations that are mathematically problematic for students. In fact, classroom lessons are organized around the solving of problems. The problems usually are drawn from a common theme or scenario for the day. Students are asked to solve the problems using the tools that are available and using whatever methods make sense to them, and then to share and discuss their methods with the class. The teacher is free to introduce methods into the discussion but does not prescribe them.

While students are first working with multidigit numbers, they are encouraged to use the physical materials. This provides a common base of experience so that all students can participate in the discussions of various solution methods. Base-ten blocks are used most consistently. After students are comfortable with the blocks, they begin using the written numerals and often manipulate the numerals to parallel the methods they are using with the blocks. Discussions center around how the methods compare. The students gradually develop more sophisticated methods with the blocks and the numerals simultaneously.

Each form of representation encourages and constrains particular kinds of solution methods. The base-ten blocks, for example, encourage regrouping methods rather than counting-on or counting-back methods. If students are solving a problem like 24 + 13 and are using base-ten blocks, they are likely to combine the tens blocks and combine the ones blocks and think, "20 and 10 is 30; 4 and 3 is 7; so the answer is 37." On the other hand, if they are not using blocks and have engaged in counting activities they may think "24, 34 (take the 10 from the 13), 35, 36, 37." Or they may count on from 24 by ones, 13 times. All of these methods are legitimate. It simply is important to note that different tools are likely to encourage different kinds of solution methods and, perhaps, different kinds of connections and understandings. The classrooms in the CBI project use base-ten blocks and, consequently, students are more likely to solve problems using a regrouping rather than a counting strategy. However, when materials (paper, pencil, blocks) are not provided, students are likely to use a variety of strategies.

The classrooms in the CBI project are located in two relatively large rural/suburban elementary schools with a wide range of ability levels. The mean achievement level of students, as measured by standardized tests, is slightly above average.

The episodes described in this chapter and the quotes from students are taken from audio/video recordings of the classroom or reconstructed from notes of the observer. One of the project directors, James Hiebert or Diana Wearne, was always present as an observer in the classrooms when the students were receiving the alternative instruction. The number of activities described in the following section represent the usual number of activities the students engaged in each day.

Ms. Devon's Class

Ms. Devon's second-grade class has thirty students with mixed achievement records. The students have been solving situations involving adding or subtracting two- and three-digit numerals for the past few weeks. The students began the year with a place value unit on numbers less than 1000. During this unit, the students were encouraged to make connections between the spoken, written, and concrete representations of quantity; each student had a set of base-ten blocks (see Figure 7–2 or 7–8 in Chapter 7). They discussed multiple ways of representing a given quantity and solved problems involving place value. The problems focused on developing an understanding of the base-ten numeration system. An example of such a problem is the following:

> Roger is working in the produce section of the market this week. He is constructing a display of apples, putting 10 apples in each row of a bin. If he started with 237 apples, how many complete rows of 10 can he make?

Most students initially solved this problem by first constructing a representation of 237 with their set of base-ten blocks (two flats, three sticks, and seven units). Some students counted how many tens were in each hundred, others traded 10 tens (sticks) for each hundred (flat), and then counted the total number of tens. Other students just thought about the number of tens in each hundred, perhaps by constructing a mental image of the hundred (flat) block. They then figured how many tens would be in two hundreds, and then added in the remaining three tens.

Another example of a problem the students solved during this unit is:

> Keisha also is working in the produce section of the store this week. The store received a shipment of oranges. Keisha's job is to record the number of oranges the store received that day. Some of the oranges are packed in crates of 100 and others are packed in boxes of 10. Keisha counted three crates of 100 and 43 boxes of 10. How many oranges did the store receive that day?

Some students solved this problem by constructing a physical representation of the situation with base-ten blocks (three flats, 43 sticks), regrouped the tens (sticks) to form groups of one hundred (flats), and then wrote the associated numeral (730). Other students used their place value understandings to know that 43 boxes of ten is 430 because 10 tens is a hundred, so 40 tens would be 400. The students then added 300 oranges from the three crates of 100 to get a total of 730 oranges.

In both of these examples the students were focusing on the *ten for one* nature of the base-ten numeration system: that there are 10 ones in each ten and 10 tens in each hundred.

The students had experiences combining two-digit numbers in first grade, but the combinations did not require regrouping. They began the current unit on adding/subtracting multidigit numbers in second grade by solving the problems with their base-ten blocks. The lessons usually began with the students being presented with a scenario for the day. The scenario might be a map of a campground with distances given between various sites in the campground, or it might be a table of information such as the lengths and heights of various dinosaurs. The students would then be asked to solve or construct problems based on the given scenario.

Prior to finding a solution to the posed question, students were asked to share the number sentences they had written to represent the given situation. Students either agreed with the given number sentence or suggested an alternative sentence. They discussed the number sentences and agreed on a single sentence or agreed that all sentences represented the situation. Ms. Devon included this activity to encourage students to think about the relationships between the story and the number sentence and to build connections between these ways of representing quantitative situations. Consider the following problem:

If a triceratops is 288 inches long and a brontosaurus is 864 inches long, how much longer is a brontosaurus than a triceratops?

Students might have constructed one of the following sentences to represent the situation: $864 - 288 = [\ ]$, or $288 + [\ ] = 864$ (written either vertically or horizontally). Discussions centered around the similarities and differences in these representations. Students then would begin working to solve the problem, often individually but with periodic conversations with neighbors about difficulties or insights.

After solving the number problem using their base-ten blocks in these early activities, the students would share their solutions with the rest of the class. Volunteers presented their methods at the chalkboard. This was accomplished by the use of large magnetized laminated paper base-ten blocks which could be displayed on the chalkboard. The students described why certain regroupings were necessary, did the regroupings, and then recorded the final answer. The students then began to record the regroupings directly on their written number sentences. The numbers became a record of the actions on the blocks. For example, if the students found they had enough tens to make another hundred, the students did the regrouping with the blocks and then recorded on their number sentence the extra hundred that they had constructed.

The students began the unit on adding and subtracting multidigit numbers in February. By mid-February, when this lesson took place, the students had begun working with just the written numbers. The students might refer to actions on the blocks, but the blocks at this point were being used primarily as an aide in explaining solutions, or as a check on computation.

Activity One

The scenario for the day's activities in Ms. Devon's class is a listing of calories in various foods from McDonald's® restaurant (McDonald's 1996). Ms. Devon obtained the list from a McDonald's restaurant and had adjusted the numbers to necessitate the need to regroup when adding or subtracting quantities, a focus of the day's lesson. For example, the calories in the hamburger was changed from 270 to 268. (Figure 8–1 is the chart Ms. Devon used with her students this day and Figure 8–2 shows the number of calories in these foods as reported by McDonald's.)

Ms. Devon posts the chart shown in Figure 8–1 and asks the students to think what they would order for lunch from McDonald's if their order contained a sandwich and a drink. Ms. Devon waits for a minute and then lists various suggestions on the chalkboard. A number of students suggest a hamburger and a coke. Ms. Devon asks the students to find the number of calories in that meal.

SANDWICHES	Calories	DRINKS	Calories	DESSERTS	Calories
Hamburger	268	Coke®	147	Apple Pie	261
Quarter Pounder®	430	Orange Drink	159	Yogurt Cone	116
Big Mac®	501	Sprite®	140	Hot Fudge Sundae	286
Filet O'Fish®	356	Chocolate Shake	337	McDonaldland® Cookies	269
Chicken McNuggets®	283	Milk	103		
		Apple Juice	85		

8–1 Calorie chart that Ms. Devon used

SANDWICHES	Calories	DRINKS	Calories	DESSERTS	Calories
Hamburger	270	Coca-Cola Classic®	150	Apple Pie	260
Quarter Pounder®	430	Hi-C Orange Drink®	160	Yogurt Cone	120
Big Mac®	530	Sprite®	150	Hot Fudge Sundae	290
Filet O'Fish®	360	Chocolate Shake	340	McDonaldland® Cookies	260
Chicken McNuggets® (6 pieces)	290	Milk	100		
		Apple Juice	80		

8–2 Calories reported by McDonald's ®

After about five minutes, the students are asked to share how they found their answer. Angela writes her number sentence on the chalkboard and then explains:

$$268$$
$$+147$$

ANGELA: Two and one makes three hundreds but I didn't write the three down because I could see that I would get another hundred from the tens. Six and four is 10 so I have enough tens to make another hundred. Now I write down the four hundreds that I have. I don't write down the zero because I can see I can get another ten from the ones. Eight and seven is 15 so that makes another ten so now I have one ten so I write that down and I have the five left over. That makes 415 calories in the lunch.

After completing her explanation, Angela looks back at her work and says:

ANGELA: I think that would have been a lot easier to explain if I had started at the other end.

Angela solved the problem from left to right, that is, combining the largest quantities (hundreds) first. Solving from left to right was the initial approach all students used in first grade for combining multidigit numbers. The students continued this approach, combining the numbers from left to right, in second grade. As the students began to solve problems involving multiple regroupings without the use of blocks, some of the students began to solve the problems from right to left, first combining the ones, then the tens, then the hundreds. Both approaches are shared in class discussion and both approaches are accepted by the students as valid approaches.

Ms. Devon believes that discussions of the different approaches are helpful for students. Rather than confusing students, comparing these different methods for addition allow students to reflect on why the methods work and to develop deeper understandings of the method they use. Ms. Devon seizes on Angela's comment as an opportunity to continue these kinds of discussions.

Ms. DEVON: What do you think Angela meant by her comment that it might have been easier to explain if she had started at the other end?

MELANIE: I think that maybe what Angela is trying to say is that you have to always explain why you didn't write down a number right away but you do it the other way, starting from the other end, you always write the number down right away. You still have to explain how you got the number, but not why you don't write it down right away.

MIKE: I did the problem the way that Angela did it only I always write down the number right away and then erase it later if I have to. Like in this problem, I wrote 2 for the hundreds and then erased it to write a 3 when I got another hundred from the tens. I don't mind erasing the number but maybe it does take more explaining.

Ms. DEVON: Who solved the problem adding from right to left? Kelly?

Kelly goes to the chalkboard to explain her solution.

KELLY: Eight and seven is 15 so I have enough ones to make another ten *(Kelly writes a one over the six in 268)* with five left over *(writes a 5 in the ones' place in the answer)*. Six and four is 10 and with the extra ten that I got from the ones, I now have 11 tens so I have enough tens to make another hundred with one ten left over *(Kelly writes a one over the two in 268 and a one in the tens' place in the answer)*. Then I add up all the hundreds and write down four. My answer is 415. That's the same as Angela's.

Activity Two

Ms. Devon continues the discussion of calories by asking which sandwich has the most calories. Christopher says it is the Big Mac®. After all the students agree, Ms. Devon asks Christopher how he decided it was the Big Mac. Christopher says it is because the Big Mac has more than 500 calories and all the rest have fewer than 500. Ms. Devon asks if anyone thought about it another way. Erin says she decided on the Big Mac because you only have to look at the biggest place, the hundreds, to decide because it takes 10 tens to make another hundred so you cannot get another hundred to be more than five. Ms. Devon asks the students what they would say to someone who thought Chicken McNuggets® had the most calories because it had an eight here (pointing to the 8 in 283) and it was larger than all the other numbers in that place. This prompts a discussion on how you would help someone with this misconception. Many students suggest that looking at a block display of the numbers might be the easiest way to show that 501 was larger than 283 because there are more blocks in 501 than in 283 because the 501 blocks have more hundreds blocks.

Ms. Devon returns the discussion to the Big Mac and asks why the Big Mac has more calories than the other sandwiches. Students come up with many suggestions, including the size (it is bigger than the other sandwiches). Ms. Devon, referring to the previous listing of choices for lunch, notes that the second most popular choice for a lunch sandwich was Chicken McNuggets. She asks the students to find how many more calories are in the Big Mac than in Chicken McNuggets.

Meredith writes a number sentence on the chalkboard she thinks tells about the problem:

$$\begin{array}{r} 501 \\ -283 \\ \hline \end{array}$$

The students agree that this sentence represents the situation. They then set to work to solve the problem.

In some ways, this problem is new for the students because it is the first time the minuend contains a zero. Students who were solving subtraction problems using something like the standard algorithm (moving from right to left, subtracting in each position) now have to regroup across a zero, a new situation for them. The students work on the problem for awhile, in pairs or by themselves. Some students work with paper and pencil for a time, then take out and work with their sets of base-ten blocks. There is more discussion than usual among neighbors. When the students appear to have finished, Ms. Devon asks for answers. The two solutions suggested are 218 and 222. Ms. Devon writes both of these on the chalkboard and then asks for a volunteer to share. Ashley volunteers and comes to the front.

ASHLEY: This was hard for me. At first I didn't know what to do. I could see I didn't have enough ones to take away three and I didn't see how to get any because there's a zero there *(pointing to the 0 in 501)*. Finally I got out my blocks and then I saw what to do. *(Ashley demonstrates her solution by representing the 501 with five flats and one little block with the large demonstration pieces.)* I saw I could get some tens from one of the hundreds so I took one of the hundreds and changed it into 10 tens. *(Ashley removes one of the flats and exchanges it for 10 sticks. She crosses off the 5 and writes a 4 on the numeral 501, and writes a 10 over the 0 in the tens' place.)* Now I have some tens so I take one of the tens and change it into 10 ones. *(Ashley removes a stick and replaces it with 10 little blocks. She crosses off the 10 and writes a 9 and writes 11 in the ones' place.)* Now I can do the subtraction. I have 11 ones and 11 take away three is eight, nine tens take away eight is one, and four hundreds take away two is two so the answer is 218 so there are 218 more calories in the Big Mac than in the Chicken McNuggets.

Ms. Devon asks if anyone has any questions for Ashley. A number of students indicate they did the same thing as Ashley, in that they used their blocks to help them. Some students seem confused but do not ask questions. Perhaps they are not sure what questions to ask. Ms. Devon asks if anyone solved the problem another way. Andrew says he did it without the blocks and comes to the front to demonstrate.

ANDREW: At first I wasn't sure what to do. I didn't have enough ones to subtract. Then I looked at the numbers and saw I could take one of the hundreds *(crosses off the 5 and writes a 4)* and change that into 10 tens *(writes a 10 in the tens' place)* and now the problem is done. Take one of the tens *(crosses off the 10 and writes a 9)*, change it into 10 ones *(writes 11 above the 1 in 501)*, and then subtract. Eleven take away three is eight, nine take away eight is one, and four take away two is two. I knew I needed a ten but there weren't any and then I thought about the blocks and then I knew what to do. I knew I could change one of the hundreds into 10 tens and then take one of those tens.

MS. DEVON: Can anyone see how someone would get the other answer, 222?

ADAM: I know because that was my answer. I knew you can't take three from one, but I couldn't see how to get any more ones because there weren't any tens so I took one from three. Now I know that I could have gotten a ten by changing one of the hundreds into 10 tens the way that Ashley did it.

Ms. Devon leads a brief discussion about Adam's last observation before moving to the next activity.

Activity Three

The last problem Ms. Devon presents on this day is:

> Jonathan had 728 calories in his lunch at McDonald's. He had a Filet O'Fish®, milk, and one other thing. What was the other thing Jonathan had in his lunch?

Ms. Devon developed this task for a number of reasons: it was a multi-step problem, she anticipated it would produce a variety of solution strategies, and she knew the students would find it interesting.

Ms. Devon treats the problem as a mystery and there is considerable excitement as students discuss with their neighbors the strategy they will use. The students work on the problem for awhile—some in pairs and some working by themselves. There is a lot of murmuring in the room and finally hands begin to go up.

Roger is one of the first students to volunteer. Roger has been experiencing difficulties in school and, although he participates in the mathematics activities, he has trouble expressing his ideas clearly and explaining his methods. Ms. Devon has worked with Roger individually, providing him with additional opportunities to talk about his thinking. Ms. Devon calls on Roger when he volunteers to share his solution.

ROGER: It was the cookies. I did it in my head and found out.

MS. DEVON: Can you tell us what you were thinking?

ROGER: I added the 356 and the 103 in my mind and got 459. Then I knew it was the cookies.

MS. DEVON: How did you know it was the cookies?

ROGER: I just knew it.

Ms. Devon thanks Roger and calls on the next volunteer, Ryan.

RYAN: I added the 356 and the 103 and got 459 *(Ryan shows his work on the chalkboard)*. I looked at the 728 and thought, um, what do I need to add to the nine to get 18 and I knew it had to be a nine. I looked at all the other things listed and the only thing with a nine in the ones' place was the cookies so I knew it had to be the cookies. I checked to make sure *(he shows how he added 269 to 459 to get 728, combining the ones first, then the tens, and then the hundreds)*.

MS. DEVON: What would you have done if there had been other foods whose caloric count ended in a nine?

RYAN: I guess I try them all because I know it has to be a nine in the ones' place.

Jessica is the next student to share her work. She writes the following on the chalkboard:

```
   728
 – 103
 – 356
```

JESSICA: I knew that if I added up the calories from the things I knew he had ordered and then subtracted from the total calories I would find the number of calories in the missing thing. Six and three is nine and I can't take nine from eight so I took one of the tens away from the two *(pointing to the 2 tens in 728, crossing off the 2 and writing a 1)* so now I have 18 and nine from 18 is nine. *(She writes the 9 in the ones' place of the missing number.)* Now I have five tens *(pointing to the tens in 356 and 103)* but I can't take five tens away from one ten so I take one of the hundreds *(crosses off the 7 and writes a 6)* so now I have 11 tens and five from 11 is six *(she writes a 6 in the tens' place in the missing number)*. Three and one is four and four from six is two so the missing thing has 269 calories. The only thing on the chart with 269 calories is the cookies. I checked my work by adding up the 356, 103, and 269 and I got 728 *(she demonstrates this on the chalkboard)*.

HOLLY: I understand what Jessica is doing, but I didn't do it that way. I added the two numbers together first and then subtracted from the 728 to get the 269 and I think that is much easier.

Other students say they agree with Holly: that you can do it Jessica's way but it is easier for them to do it Holly's way. Ms. Devon asks if anyone solved it a different way.

ERIC: I added up the 356 and the 103 and got 459. I noticed that Jonathan didn't have a dessert. First I tried the apple pie and that didn't work. Then I tried the yogurt cone and that didn't work. Then I tried the hot fudge sundae and that didn't work. Then I tried the cookies and that worked!

Discussion

The five dimensions described in Chapters 2–6 (and shown in Figure 1–1) are clearly at work in shaping the nature of this lesson. All of them contributed to build an environment in which children were encouraged to make connections. We would like to highlight three dimensions that seemed to play a prominent role here: the nature of the task, the role of the teacher, and the influence of mathematical tools. If we had reported on another day in Ms. Devon's class, other dimensions may have come to the fore.

The Nature of Tasks

The lesson began with students deciding what they would like for lunch at a fast-food restaurant. This setting provided a chance for students to help in generating a problem to solve. Ms. Devon selected a task from their suggestions that included the regrouping features she wanted students to grapple with in this lesson.

The second task was to determine how many more calories were in one sandwich than another. The purpose of this task was to provide a new experience for students who were using a right-to-left subtraction procedure, regrouping across a zero. Students regularly encountered new situations for which they needed to modify their current procedures or develop new ones, so Ms. Devon did not engage in the traditional warning about a new kind of problem or suggest that it might be more difficult. She expected that some students would need multiple opportunities to solve problems like this over a number of days, but wanted to begin the discussions today as she always did—with students' suggestions.

The third task was a multistep problem that included a number of regrouping situations and could be solved in a wide variety of ways. Ms. Devon felt that this would be a good concluding activity for the day and that students would find it intriguing. It should provide multiple opportunities to compare solution methods.

All three tasks illustrate the critical features of tasks introduced in Chapter 1 and described in Chapter 2. The mathematics was problematic for the students. Depending on the student's level of understanding and skill, different problems may have been more challenging than others. But for no students were all three tasks routine exercises, and for no students were all three tasks inaccessible.

Given the students' background and the nature of the previous activities, the tasks connected quite naturally with what students had been doing before. Students had already developed computation methods that they could use to begin solving the problems so the problems were within reach. Depending on the student's methods, some adjustments may have been required. But all students were in a good starting position.

Finally, the tasks were chosen so that something of mathematical value might be left behind. Some students were beginning to use the standard algorithms quite regularly and Ms. Devon wanted these students to think about how these methods could be extended and used flexibly to solve problems that made somewhat different computational demands. Beyond the fact that the students had shown considerable enthusiasm for discussions about fast-food products and Ms. Devon expected the students to be interested in the scenarios, the tasks were chosen carefully for the kinds of mathematics in which students would be engaged.

The Role of the Teacher

Ms. Devon's perception of her role as a teacher permeated all aspects of the lesson. We will underscore two features of her role: guiding the mathematical activities, and helping to establish the social culture of the classroom. Ms. Devon guided students' mathematical activities both in planning the lesson and in interacting with the students during the lesson. Selecting the tasks provided a powerful way for Ms. Devon to direct students' attention to particular kinds of mathematical situations, and over time, to provide students with the opportunities to establish mathematical relationships and take with them particular kinds of competencies. During the lesson, Ms. Devon took advantage of Angela's comment that it would have been easier to explain if she had used a different method to redirect students' attention to various features of the methods they were using, to think about how they were alike and different.

A central feature of the social culture of this classroom is that *methods of solution serve as the currency of conversation*. Class discussions revolve around methods for solving problems and students pick up on the idea that developing better methods—methods that they understand—is a primary goal in mathematics. Given Ms. Devon's continual focus on the methods used to solve problems, it is not hard to see how such a culture has been established.

It is interesting to note that guiding the mathematical activities of students and helping to establish the social culture of the classroom often overlap. When Ms. Devon encouraged the continued discussion of Angela's left-to-right versus right-to-left method, she was moving the mathematical discussion in a particular direction and also reaffirming that the analysis of methods is a conversation topic of value. This overlap is not surprising because, as we have argued previously, instruction is a system. If teachers take seriously some of the features in the system we are describing, the others come along. All of the critical features work together.

Mathematical Tools as Learning Supports

By this time in second grade, most students were solving the problems with pencil and paper. In order to uncover the influence of tools in shaping the way these students thought about addition and subtraction and the kinds of methods they were using we need to back up a bit. Many of the students had used base-ten blocks when they were first developing methods to add and subtract multidigit numbers. The most common methods, and the ones that received most discussion in class, were built from decomposing numbers into tens and ones (or hundreds, tens, and ones), combining these units, and then recomposing the parts. These methods move quite naturally into the standard algorithms and many students were now using methods that looked quite like these standard algorithms.

When the students decided to subtract to find how many more calories one sandwich had than another, they were faced with the problem 501 – 273. A number of students went back to the base-ten blocks. Some students worked out the problem using the blocks, but some students laid out just five flats and one small cube (or, in some cases, just one flat), looked at them for a moment, and then said to themselves, "Oh, I know," and began working with pencil and paper. It is this last group that illustrates most clearly the way in which tools can support and shape students' thinking. These students had established close relationships between the blocks and the written numbers. They were visualizing the blocks, using the blocks to guide their thinking, and then working out a written method based on these block-supported ideas.

It is important to remember that students were able to use the blocks as tools for thought because they were very familiar with them and had used them for some time. Tools are not likely to support students' thinking if they are used only for a short time or if they are used only for demonstrations. As noted in Chapter 5, students must become handy using tools and this takes time.

Conclusion

Ms. Devon's classroom is different in some ways from the classrooms pictured in the surrounding chapters. It is even different in some ways from the other classrooms in the CBI project. What is important, however, is that the differences are about things we believe are optional. Classrooms that support students' understanding can look quite different on the surface. However, what is equally important is that a deeper search shows that these classrooms share many of the same features. We believe that the shared features are exactly those described in Chapters 1–6 and summarized in Figure 1–1. In each classroom episode, a different subset of these features may be most evident. However, if one observed in Ms. Devon's classroom for any length of time, or in the other classrooms described in this book, or if one looks across the classrooms described in Chapters 7–10, it is this core set of classroom features that continually reappear.

9 *Student Talk in a Problem-Centered Classroom*

The Problem Centered Learning (PCL) approach to teaching mathematics project is directed by Piet Human, Hanlie Murray, and Alwyn Olivier at the University of Stellenbosch in South Africa. This is a large, multifaceted project including curriculum development and teacher training. A focus of the initial work was addition and subtraction of multidigit numbers, but it has expanded well beyond that now.

Computation is viewed as a vehicle that students can use to increase their understanding of number and the properties of numbers and operations. In problem-centered learning classrooms, students are presented with computation problems that are meaningful and interesting to them, but which they cannot solve with ease using routinized procedures or drilled responses. The teacher does not demonstrate a solution method, nor does the teacher indicate a preferred method, yet she or he expects every student to become involved with the problem and to attempt to solve it. Students' own invented methods are expected and encouraged. It is expected of students to discuss, critique, explain, and when necessary, justify their interpretations and solutions.

Students use methods for solving addition and subtraction problems that are based directly on their conceptions of number. Learning activities for number topics are aimed at helping students construct increasingly sophisticated meanings for number. For young children, a number like 37 means only 37 single objects. There is no understanding of the number in terms of tens and ones. Later, students realize they can make 37 by counting by tens (10, 20, 30) and then counting 7 ones. Still later, they see that 37 is made up of 3 tens and 7 ones. These are major conceptual developments and the goal of instruction is to help students experience these developments. Young students in PCL classrooms engage in a variety of counting activities. They count large sets of objects into groups, beads on a ten-frame, and numbers on a hundreds-chart. They become especially skilled at counting in tens. Consequently, many of their invented addition and subtraction methods are based on counting. The way in which students build their procedures from their conceptions of number is therefore somewhat different from students in some of the other projects described here, who develop addition and subtraction methods by building from their manipulations of physical materials.

Computation activities in the PCL classrooms involve presenting small groups of students with a word problem. Students are expected to work individually or as a group to develop a method to solve the problem and then to present their method to their peers and the teacher. The teacher provides suggestions for notation and terminology when needed, but does not demonstrate particular solution methods. By reflecting on the methods of others and working out ways of communicating their own methods, students are expected to develop increasingly advanced conceptions of number.

In the upper elementary grades (fourth grade and higher) topics such as common and decimal fractions are presented similarly, the main difference being that teachers find it more difficult to construct suitable tasks (learning environments) for these topics than for whole number computation.

In the classroom, different events may occur in different sequences. The teacher may elect to work with only part of her or his class, or the teacher may work with the whole class. These decisions are influenced by the ages of the students, the number of students in the class, and the mathematics that she or he wishes to address. Presenting students with a challenging problem which they are expected to solve without teacher assistance is the most frequently used learning episode.

When the students are slightly older (e.g., fourth grade and onward) a popular operation is for the teacher to pose a problem to the whole class, make sure that they understand the problem, and then ask them to continue. While students are solving the problem they are expected to interact with each other in whatever fashion they need at a particular point in the problem-solving process. For example, some students may initially work individually and only after having reached a tentative solution feel the need for discussion and sharing; at other times they may choose to discuss the problem first, reach consensus about a solution method, and then proceed as above.

During the problem-solving phase, interaction among students is informal and voluntary, its form dictated by the nature of the task (and especially its level of difficulty) and the individual student's needs. Students may be working in pairs or in clusters of four, assigned by the teacher or according to the students' choices. Since the groups are not cooperative learning groups in the sense that each group is required to reach consensus on an answer, many teachers do not make use of any physical grouping structure, but simply encourage students to move around and talk to or collaborate with whom they wish. The main emphasis is on *personal* construction of meaning within a community which supports discourse and the construction of shared meanings: the process of constructing shared meanings should not be perceived as more desirable than (and occurring at the expense of) personal understanding (Murray, Olivier, and Human 1993). Social interaction is seen as conducive to personal construction in that it encourages reflection, the identification and correction of mistakes, and the development of concepts.

While students are solving the problem, the teacher moves among them, but limits her or his role to that of facilitator. When some students have solved the problem, the teacher may give those students a new problem. When everybody has solved the first problem, the teacher may initiate a general class discussion on the different methods used, or decisions taken and the nature and reasons for some mistakes students may have made. This general discussion has a more formal nature than the student interaction which takes place while the problem is being solved.

For some problems, students work on their own (independently of the teacher) for a considerable length of time. What happens when PCL students are working on their own? What is the quality of young students' mathematical thinking when they are working independently in peer groups?

To investigate this question we videotaped several groups of students in the classroom who were left solving mathematical problems on their own. All of these sessions showed a similar pattern of development and similar interaction patterns among the students themselves. Therefore, it seems fair to assume that these episodes are typical of those classrooms where similar social contracts have been established. Videotaped recordings and personal observations of other classrooms bear this out.

A Problem-Solving Session

The following session consisting of four students solving a problem without teacher intervention was recorded in a fourth-grade classroom during the eighth month of the school year. The school is situated in a large country town. The teacher, Ms. Lombard, has taught at the school for many years and has participated in inservice teacher education sessions for PCL during the past five years. These sessions took the form of a small number of short workshops organized by the local education authority, followed by a program of quarterly meetings initiated by the teachers in the area. During these meetings teachers share ideas about matters like resources and assessment. Ms. Lombard uses a textbook designed for problem-centered learning as her main source of tasks. She regards this class as of above average ability, and the students recorded in this session as average for the class.

The class period was fifty minutes long. The recorded session lasted forty minutes. Ms. Lombard presented the following problem verbally to the class: Mom makes small apple tarts, using three-quarters of an apple for each small tart. She has 20 apples. How many small apple tarts can she make?

Ms. Lombard selected this problem so that students could become familiar with its structure (a grouping or measurement type of division problem where the group size is a fraction). Many students and even adults cannot solve this problem when they are required to identify the operation and perform it $(20 \div 3/4)$ to reach a solution. Yet this problem can be solved in a variety of ways through a variety of strategies when students are encouraged to analyze the physical situation and construct methods that fit their interpretation of the situation. A class discussion of these different conceptualizations of the problem and the methods that are based on them help students to gain a deeper understanding of the problem.

The students started working on the problem in small voluntary groups. Ms. Lombard sometimes withdrew completely to work at her desk, and at other times moved around in the classroom, asking questions and challenging students. One of the groups of students was videotaped. (Ms. Lombard was requested not to approach them.) This is a transcription of the videotape. The few instances in which the conversation on the tape was not clearly audible have been omitted.

During the first phase, lasting about fifteen minutes, there is comparatively little conversation and little interaction; the students would often think aloud. For example:

NINA: This is going to take too long—Ouch! SSh!

JEANETTE: This is going to take too long.

NINA: I mean this way is going to take too long. I think I'd better take another way. Have you got the answer?

(Laughter)

NINA: Twenty apples, so that's at least twenty milk tarts. . . . But now, she has—Oh, I got the answer!

JEANETTE: Will you please just keep quiet.

NINA: Almost, almost . . . I just have to add it up.

Each student then gives the answer that she has obtained, and Jeanette and Nina explain their methods. Although Nina has made an obvious and common computational error, the other three students are so uninvolved at this stage that they do not notice it, and an impasse is reached. The video recording shows feelings of helplessness and amusement at their predicament. The discussion preceding this point went as follows:

NINA: OK, Kerri, what's your answer?

KERRI: No, Liz, what's yours?

JEANETTE: I got that she could make fifteen apple tarts.

KERRI: So did I.

LIZ: Because what I did twenty divided by 4 to find out what one-third is . . . a fourth is, and then I timesed it by three and I got fifteen.

NINA: It's the wrong way, I think.

KERRI: What did you do?

NINA: See I—what I did she has twenty apples. She only needs three-quarters to make one apple tart, so she should at least make twenty apple tarts . . . OK.

(Laughter)

NINA: If you don't understand that, don't worry. Then there are twenty apples left, twenty quarters left over, and so I thought I would take *three* . . . plus three plus three plus three plus three plus three and I got eighteen, and I plussed the eighteen and the twenty and got 38 as my answer.

The error Nina makes here is to take the sum of the six threes as the answer to 20÷3, instead of the *number* of threes.

KERRI: So they could make 38 apple tarts.

NINA: That's what I got. Don't you agree?

JEANETTE: Twelve . . . three-quarters. Three-quarters plus three-quarters is equal to one and a half.

NINA: You can go three times four is twelve.

JEANETTE: Oh, I see what was my mistake

LIZ: Why did you say that they got twenty apple tarts?

NINA: Well you see twenty here, milk tarts, I wrote as opposed to apple tarts, she's got to use three-quarters of an apple tart, of an apple to make an apple tart, you understand that. She can at least make twenty.

KERRI: But how do you know she can at least make twenty?

NINA: Because she has twenty apples. You don't seem to understand me. And then twenty quarters left over so another three-fourths are going to make one apple tart, so plus three plus three plus three plus three plus three plus three is eighteen, plus eighteen plus twenty is 38.

KERRI: I don't quite follow your method.

NINA: Well . . . what do we do next?

LIZ: I don't know.

After some time, the deadlock is broken by Liz.

LIZ: Must I explain my method to you again?

Here follows some very polite but, at first glance, not very mathematically productive conversation:

LIZ: Well, what have *you* done? Because maybe yours is the right way.

NINA: I think your answers are wrong but mine might not be right.

JEANETTE: She's got a point there.

Immediately after this Nina suggests that they draw the apples, which they all start doing, although with some protest. This seems to indicate that the preceding few minutes' polite exchanges actually did prepare them to involve themselves with the problem.

A phase of intense activity starts. Only at this point does it seem as if the real thinking and argument take off.

NINA: Should we draw the apples?

LIZ: *You* can draw them.

NINA: One apple, one apple . . . I think we should just draw one apple.

KERRI: You don't have to do many.

NINA: Three-quarters of an apple.

LIZ: I'll do it as well.

JEANETTE: Guys, I've got twenty-three.

KERRI: Twenty-three? But how did you get that?

KERRI: I'm going to work it out again.

NINA: Mine is right! I've worked it out! My answer is right!

KERRI: But how do you know, because you've only drawn one apple!

NINA: But I've worked it out! Look, I'll show you—here, see, I've used that three and there's one left, twenty apples and one left. So there are twenty of that.

KERRI: I think you've got yours right, but I'm just going to work it out again to see. . . . How did you get—

LIZ: I think I've got the answer and our answer might be wrong.

KERRI: I'm listening.

JEANETTE: In each apple there is a quarter left. In each apple there is a quarter left, so you've used, you've made twenty tarts already and you've got a quarter of twenty see—

LIZ: So you've got twenty quarters *left*.

JEANETTE: Yes, . . . and twenty quarters is equal to five apples, . . . so five apples divided by—

LIZ: Six, seven, eight.

JEANETTE: By three-quarters equals three.

KERRI: But she can't make only three apple tarts!

JEANETTE: No, you've still got twenty.

LIZ: But you've got twenty quarters, if you've got twenty quarters you might be right.

JEANETTE: I'll show you.

LIZ: No, I've drawn them all here.

KERRI: How many quarters have you got? Twenty?

LIZ: Yes, one quarter makes five apples and out of five apples she can make five tarts which will make that twenty-five tarts and then she will have, wait, one, two, three, four, five quarters, she'll have one, two, three, four, five quarters. . . .

NINA: I've got a better . . .

KERRI: Yes?

LIZ: Twenty-six quarters and a remainder of one quarter left.

Nina remains outside this discussion, because she still believes that she has the correct solution. She was the only one who originally interpreted the structure of the problem correctly, but made a computational error. It may be that her knowledge that the others' original interpretations were definitely wrong now prevents her from being willing to listen to them.

Nina tries to rejoin the discussion, but the other three seem to have established consensus about the basic correctness of their approach and Liz and Jeanette are trying to construct a coherent explanation for Kerri's benefit, who is listening intently.

NINA: I've got another way, see my answer will be wrong because that is *eighteen*, minus four, so that is fourteen, that's one whole, minus four is ten minus four is six minus four is two, OK? Then I have a remainder of two apples but I have an answer of one whole, two wholes, three wholes, four wholes, I've got four wholes, it's twenty-four remainder two.

Nina is now trying to make whole apples from the remaining quarters, but takes 18 as the number of remaining quarters and not 20. The other three students are so involved in their own discussion that they are not prepared to listen to her at this point. Liz has formulated exactly the same strategy of dealing with the remaining quarters, but (correctly) using 20 quarters:

LIZ: No, can I show you my way?

NINA: Or 38.

LIZ: What I've done, I've done all those then you've got twenty quarters left, then you do twenty divided by one-fourth and you get five apples.

NINA: Twenty-four.

LIZ: But then I'll have five apples left if you put them all together.

KERRI: What? Explain again.

LIZ: Twenty divided by one-quarter would make it five quarters. So then, she'd make one tart and she'd have two quarters left over which would make it twenty-one. . . .

NINA: Don't change your answers now, just leave them how they are.

Nina is clearly not willing to listen.

LIZ: But I understand where I went wrong so she could only make twenty-one.

KERRI: Look, I've drawn twenty apples.

NINA: But she could make twenty-four.

KERRI: Why?

JEANETTE: Guys, can I explain?

KERRI: Yes?

JEANETTE: See, you've got twenty apples—You only use three-quarters of one apple so you obviously have to have more than twenty.

KERRI: Oh, yes. Look, I must color mine.

JEANETTE: You've got twenty quarters left and twenty divided by one-fourth is equal to five.

LIZ: Which would make it five apples.

JEANETTE: Yes, it's right, it's five *apples*.

LIZ: So she could make twenty-four tarts and she'd have a remainder of one quarter. Yes.

JEANETTE: *No* . . . a remainder of two quarters.

LIZ: Because look here, if you take the five apples . . .

Jeanette: You've got twenty quarters.

LIZ: Yes.

JEANETTE: So she can make twenty-five apple tarts.

NINA: I *still* think she can make twenty-four remainder two.

LIZ: You've done all the apples and you'd have twenty apple tarts and you'd have twenty quarters left over and now if you divide the twenty into quarters then you'd have five full apples, and five full apples you can make five tarts and then another one from the left-over quarters and then you'd have a remainder of two quarters.

JEANETTE: Just hold on. . . . I know what's wrong . . . one, two, three, four, five.

LIZ: Do you see?

KERRI: Not *exactly*.

JEANETTE: . . . And you've still got one, two, three, four, five quarters. So you've already made twenty-five, you've still got five quarters and here you only use three quarters so you can make *twenty-six* remainder two.

LIZ: Yes.

JEANETTE: And you have half left, and you can store it in your Deepfreeze or your refrigerator or you—

NINA: I still say twenty-four remainder two quarters, remainder two *quarters*, *then* you say *twenty-five* remainder two quarters, no, *now* you say *twenty-six* remainder two quarters, now what next?

This last (possibly sarcastic) remark of Nina's elicits a direct response from Liz and Jeanette, but Nina counters with another sarcastic remark, and Nina then turns to Kerri, who has committed herself to trying to understand their reasoning.

LIZ: Here you've got the apples and you cut them into quarters, into three quarters and you can make tarts and then you've got twenty quarters left over and then you do twenty quarters . . . .

JEANETTE: And then you've got twenty quarters, that's twenty divided by one-fourth is equal to five.

LIZ: So you've got five full apples, and then you can make . . . oopsie . . . and then you can make five apple tarts with those five and you can make another one with the quarters, with the remainder of . . .

NINA: But there's six quarters left.

LIZ: Do you see it's twenty-six remainder two?

NINA: Do you want to hear all the answers—fifteen, thirty-eight, twenty-two remainder two quarters, twenty-four remainder two quarters, twenty-five remainder two quarters and twenty-six remainder two quarters!

LIZ: But do you understand why you have twenty-six remainder two quarters?

KERRI: No, but I get twenty, twenty, one, two, three, four, five, then—

LIZ: Then you've got five quarters left over.

JEANETTE: Yes, but then you've got five quarters left so that you can make another one. So then you've got a remainder of a half an apple.

KERRI: Yeah.

Discussion

As described in the previous chapters, there are certain features of classrooms that determine the nature of a learning episode like the one described and that account for its success. We will highlight several features that follow along these dimensions: the nature of the task, the role of the teacher, and the social culture of the classroom.

The Nature of the Task

An episode like this is initiated and sustained by tasks that are genuine problems for students, tasks that offer opportunities for students to perceive problems that they need to solve. The task provides the opportunity, but the students must set the goal of completing the task for the task to become problematic. In this episode, students were initially following the teacher's instructions to solve the problem. They had not really adopted this goal as their own. But shortly after the point where Nina suggests that they draw the apples, they show that they have taken ownership of the problem and have made a personal commitment to solve it. It is only at this point that they begin to seriously reflect on the mathematics of the task.

In many traditional mathematics classrooms, it is unusual for fourth graders to work together on solving a problem for forty minutes—or even ten minutes. Most problems can be solved quite quickly, in two or three minutes or less. What enables students to work for prolonged periods of time solving a single problem? An appropriate task is surely part of the reason. The task of apples and tarts, although not fancy or elaborate, connected well with students' current level of functioning. They understood the task and already had developed some methods with which they could begin, but the task was challenging and their methods needed to be rethought and reshaped. It is a mistake, though, to think that the task alone encourages students to work for forty minutes. Teachers who simply change tasks will not find students suddenly working independently for long periods of time. Other dimensions of this instructional system, such as the role of the teacher and the social culture of the classroom, are equally important.

The Role of the Teacher

After the teacher has presented a suitable task, she or he should allow the students to work on the task without continual interruptions and interference. Even teachers who wholeheartedly accept this as a principle do not always realize the extent to which students can be trusted to resolve their own dilemmas while they are struggling with a problem.

Many teachers may have felt compelled to intervene in this episode and resolve Nina's doubts by pressing for consensus, but constructing mathematical knowledge and reaching true understanding are deeply personal processes which are very sensitive to interferences. A lack of time and a quiet space in which to think may delay these processes. Since Nina was the first student to grasp the basic structure of the problem and actually set the others off on the right track, it seems amazing that she could not reach the correct answer. Her way of dealing with the remaining 20 quarters was initially quite different from theirs—she wanted to find the number of threes in twenty, whereas they put together 20 quarters to make whole apples. When Nina decided to use this approach as well, the other students were not aware of it. It is possible that if Nina had allowed herself some more time for reflection, she would have been able to correct her error.

This sensitivity to the process of constructing knowledge and understanding is illustrated even more powerfully by the way the impasses are dealt with. The students' progress came to an apparent standstill two or three times in the course of solving the problem, and although these periods lasted for several minutes, the students themselves broke the impasse each time. We have observed that many teachers have a low threshold of tolerance for this type of situation, and want to intervene with a suggestion to get a group going again. Many teachers feel it is their responsibility to clear up immediately any confusion and remove any obstacle to progress. This episode suggests that teachers should think carefully before they intervene—students may frequently be able to resolve impasses by themselves. By intervening too often or too quickly teachers may undermine the social culture they are trying to build.

The Social Culture of the Classroom

A feature that heavily influenced this episode is the social contract which underlies the interactions between students and teacher and, in this case, between student and student. The episode illustrates many of the points made in Chapter 4; we will review two of them here.

The first point to consider is the importance of mistakes: Mistakes are sites for learning. As Nina observed sarcastically, the whole episode is studded with incorrect answers. These wrong answers sometimes were simply the result of incomplete or ill-formed thinking, but sometimes they served as stepping stones as students built their solutions. One might even say that a learning sequence of the kind in the episode would be unlikely without the mistakes that occurred along the way. The mistakes often signaled differences in students' opinions and these differences generated the arguments and the attempts to justify and explain. And these justifications and explanations provided the real learning opportunities, both for the speaker and for the listeners.

The second feature to consider is how communication skills develop and enable further learning. This episode illustrates how students use mathematical language to communicate. Through much of the episode, students used mathematically incorrect language. Phrases like "twenty divided by a quarter give five" were common. This does not seem to have hampered their communication, possibly because they still had the physical situation in mind. Eventually, though, the students themselves experienced the need to express their thoughts as clearly and coherently as possible. In the end, the (correct) solution method is described four times, with increasing clarity and conviction.

Even when students are sure that they have reached the correct answer, and know how they have reached it, they need to articulate their thinking repeatedly. In this episode it can be argued that the explanations were for Kerri's benefit, but there is a strong impression that the explanations actually served to stabilize the speaker's own conceptions. It is common for students in problem-centered classrooms to engage in explanations and justifications to promote reflection and to establish a social culture of intellectual risk taking, a tolerance for mistakes, and of mutual respect. However, this episode illustrates how strongly students themselves need to construct a coherent, exact account of their thinking. As Lampert (in press) has noted, understanding something is at least partly a function of helping others understand it.

Conclusion

During this forty-minute episode, four students who are familiar with inquiry learning and have participated in the system of instruction we are describing try to solve a problem through personal engagement, argument, and reflection. They feel free to hold their own opinions, change their minds, build on others' thinking, invent their own methods, and adopt the methods of others. This is all a natural part of the problem-solving process.

Earlier we asked the question "What happens when students are working on their own?" The episode illustrates what can happen and our observations suggest that the episode is typical for students in the kinds of classrooms we have described. What this means is that students can reason mathematically and construct important understandings without teacher intervention. This should not be interpreted as a conclusion that teachers should never intervene, nor is it a conclusion that this is the only kind of learning situation that is productive. Rather, the conclusion is that students can take responsibility for their own learning provided the task is suitable and the social culture is of such a nature that students know this kind of behavior is expected. The message is that students can work well independently and teachers should not assume too quickly that intervention is the best choice.

10 *Snapshots Across Two Years in the Life of an Urban Latino Classroom*

In this chapter we will follow a class of first graders through first and second grade, observing them in typical lessons.[1] The lesson topics have been selected to demonstrate key aspects of classrooms that support understanding. The lessons and approaches come from the last set of classroom teaching experiments in the Supporting Ten-Structured Thinking (STST) project directed by Karen Fuson at Northwestern University. These studies were funded under a National Science Foundation project called Latino Children's Constructions of Arithmetical Understandings in Urban Classrooms That Support Thinking. This project focused on word problems, single-digit addition and subtraction methods that use ten, and multidigit addition and subtraction in grades 1 and 2. We also did some work in kindergarten and third grade. Curriculum materials (*Children's Math Worlds*) were developed over a three-year period. We worked with children in both English-speaking and Spanish-speaking classes. Most children are from Spanish-speaking backgrounds, but some children are African American and some are European American.

The Project Approach

We begin the year with two major foci: One is decomposing numbers below ten into many possible pairs of numbers (often set within sharing situations). The other is generation of mathematical stories by children that are then mathematized by the teacher into various simple kinds of word problems. Children show numbers to themselves and to others with objects, fingers, and mathematical drawings (simplifications of the situation into dots, circles, etc.). Decomposition allows children to begin seeing flexible combinations of numbers that compose other numbers. They also can see relations between pairs and overall patterns. Decomposition also helps children learn the basic addition/subtraction facts below ten in a related way. Finally, decomposition allows children to begin building one of the prerequisites for ten-structured methods of addition and subtraction: being able to break a number into a given number and the rest. Eliciting mathematical stories from children allows the teacher to get to know the children (because most of the children's stories are about themselves and their families). These stories relate early mathematical processing to children's lives, and they facilitate children's mathematical understanding because the situations are familiar and engaging.

We help children learn how to use their fingers to show numbers in the mathematical story situations. Fingers are an inexpensive, powerful, and natural tool for problem solving. Children in almost all cultures learn to use their fingers to solve numerical situations. There is a progression of more advanced finger methods that children use if they have frequent opportunities to use their fingers in mathematical class. Our experience with many different classes of children is that fingers do not become a crutch that slows children down in later grades. When we help children move on to more advanced methods, many children do not need fingers by third grade. The few who still need them have rapid and reliable finger addition and subtraction methods. Many children from Latin American countries, and from other parts of the world, put numbers on their fingers in ways different from the typical method in the United States (raising the index finger first and the thumb last). All of these methods can be accepted, and all children can be helped to move on to more advanced methods (see Fuson [1992] for a description of these methods).

Our word problem work begins with the simplest kinds of addition, subtraction, multiplication, and division (equal sharing) problems. Children show these situations with drawn dots, circles, and fingers. Children tell word problems, and they solve problems posed by other children and by the teacher. Later children solve, tell, and write more difficult problems in which the unknown is not the final quantity. Traditional mathematical tools such as number sentences are introduced during this time, but children use them to show *the situation*—not the solution method. We also use problems with irrelevant information and two-step problems. Over time, numbers in the problems also increase in size, but we keep numbers in more difficult problems smaller than those in simple problems.

Another method is to give a situation involving several different numbers and ask children to pose many different questions about that situation. Children also pose and solve problems about information graphs, and they make graphs. Thus, children do a lot of problem posing, question asking, and describing of their problem-solving methods. They also solve a much richer range of problem types than is typical in most textbooks (see Fuson [1992] for a description). This whole approach emphasizes thinking about the underlying situation and then mathematizing that situation (stripping it down to its mathematical elements).

We introduce tens and ones and how to write two-digit numbers by having children use penny strips that show ten pennies. A dime is shown on the back to clarify the meaning of a dime as ten pennies. Children use the penny strips to learn to count to 100 by tens and by ones. They also record the penny strips by drawing columns of ten circles. Later they draw a line through the column to show the strip, and still later just draw the stick as a ten. Children use penny strips and drawn ten-sticks and circles (ones) for multidigit adding and subtracting.

Children initially use penny strips or draw columns of tens or ten-sticks when adding and subtracting multidigit numbers. Penny strips allow children to work with the meanings they have. Some children count by ones, and others count by tens (10, 20, 30, 40, 50) or count the tens (1, 2, 3, 4, 5 tens). Both of these ways of thinking of tens have been built up by activities in which children count in each of these ways and read a number such as 53 as both fifty-three and five tens and three ones. By the end of first grade, almost all children can use addition methods involving tens, not just ones. Many children also invent mental methods that do not use penny strips or drawn quantities, and by the end of second grade most children do two-digit and three-digit multidigit addition and subtraction using numbers (and perhaps fingers). The purpose of all of this work is that children understand the number words and written multidigit numbers as collections of thousands, hundreds, tens, and ones. Unless these meanings are very strong, children may begin to use methods based on how the numbers look instead of what they mean. Children make many errors when they see multidigit numbers as separate ones digits.

Children develop their own methods of multidigit adding and subtracting using tens and ones. They explain their methods to other children, try to use other children's methods, and compare different methods. These all help children to reflect on their own and on others' methods. The latter two kinds of activities also ensure that children listen to and try to understand other children's methods. Solving problems in different ways is emphasized, but children in different classes sometimes have certain kinds of methods that dominate. This frequently is because the activities in that class have enabled the children to think more rapidly in one way than in another (e.g., counting by tens might be emphasized). We have found that different children do have preferences for different methods even within the same class, so we view it as important that the teacher support different ways of thinking about multidigit addition and subtraction problems. Such different methods also enable children to build more complex and generalizable understandings of multidigit situations. Children who are making errors are helped by peers or the teacher with whatever part of their process they are doing wrong.

The examples of classroom activities in this chapter have more formal structured activities in the beginning, when children have to construct initial mathematical knowledge. Later activities demonstrate the varied ways in which children use the knowledge they constructed in such activities. In all activities, the teacher tries to set expectations that children will be active and autonomous learners and that they have responsibilities to share their own thinking and to help their classmates develop their own thinking.

The Examples Chosen

To compose this chapter, we selected examples from our English-speaking and Spanish-speaking classes to give readers some sense of major aspects of our approach. These examples are typical of many of our past classes and children. We changed the names to make one hypothetical class to follow through two years. Some vignettes are taken verbatim from videotapes, and others are constructed from classroom observation notes. We have not included all of the bumps and glitches of ordinary urban classes of inner-city children (e.g., interruptions), and we portray a teacher who has created a safe and nourishing learning environment. Furthermore, informal activities that arise from children, and discussions of children's thinking, can sometimes go extraordinarily well. Substantial insights may be made by several or many participants, often including the teacher. Sometimes such discussions do not go well. Things may get muddled or tangential. We have avoided examples of either of these extremes.

In this chapter we initially see this class near the beginning of first grade. The class of twenty-four children has a wide range of mathematical knowledge, but most can count to ten and write the numerals one through nine. A few can count to 100, but most cannot. Some of the children have not had any preschool or kindergarten experience. The teacher is working to identify someone in each home to help with mathematical homework every day. She has spoken to some of the parents of the children who cannot count or write numbers to ten about helping their child at home and plans to continue making such parent contacts. She also is trying to organize some time for a teacher aide to work with these children during school. The teacher has been using word problems as a way to get to know her children and their mathematical knowledge. She tries to adapt word problems that come from the children to her mathematical goals.

Classroom Vignettes

End of First Week of School

Ms. Lo Cicero: Roberto, come and share with the class a story. A story about you. Be sure to speak loud and clear so we may all hear. Students, please listen carefully to Roberto's story because I will ask questions to see how well you can remember his story.

Roberto: In Mexico I have a dog. My dog's name is Paco. My uncle takes care of the dog. He feeds him bones and water. When I visit Mexico, I play with him.

Ms. Lo Cicero: Great story! Roberto, how many bones does your uncle feed him?

Roberto: He feeds him five bones every day.

Ms. Lo Cicero: If yesterday your uncle fed him five bones and today he feeds him another five bones, how many bones does he eat in two days?

Roberto: Five. *(Some students say ten.)*

Ms. Lo Cicero: Can you go and draw this on the board?

Roberto goes to the board and draws five bones and, after a space, another five bones.

Ms. Lo Cicero: Ah! So five one day and five another day. Could you please draw the dishes your uncle uses to feed Paco? Draw the plates around the bones.

Roberto: You want me to put the bones on plates?

Ms. Lo Cicero: Yes, Roberto.

Roberto encircles each group with one plate.

Ms. Lo Cicero: Roberto, ask the classroom questions about your story. *(Silence)*

Ms. Lo Cicero: Who would like to ask a question about the story? Yes, Karina.

Karina: What was the dog's name?

Ms. Lo Cicero: Very good. Karina, choose a student to answer your question.

Karina chooses Sandra.

SANDRA: Paco.

MS. LO CICERO: Now *you* can ask a question.

The teacher helps students ask questions that other students answer: Who feeds the dog? Where does Paco live? How many bones does he get?

MS. LO CICERO: Class, answer the questions I am going to ask by showing me with your fingers. Now pay attention to the questions we are going to ask about the story. How many groups of bones do we have here?

Most say ten. Only three show two fingers.

MS. LO CICERO: Listen to the question, "How many *groups* of bones do we have here? How many dishes do we have with bones in them?" *(relating the mathematical question to the real-world story).*

Most students show two fingers.

MS. LO CICERO: How many bones did Paco eat in two days?

Most students show ten fingers.

These two questions are then asked several times to several individual students to be sure they were listening and understanding. The teacher then asks another child to tell a story and another discussion ensues.

The Next Day

While students are playing in the playground, the teacher draws 17 bones on the board. She plans to continue Roberto's story but to use it as a transition to the topic of the day. The focus today is to discuss various kinds of groupings that occur in the world, and to examine various decompositions of the number eight. When the students come in, the class talks about yesterday's lesson, reviewing some parts of the story. ·

MS. LO CICERO: Without counting, just by looking at all these bones, can anyone try to guess how many bones I drew here?

MOST STUDENTS: 20, 22, 13. *(One student counted quickly and said 17.)*

MS. LO CICERO: You all made very good guesses. Chantelli, you counted them really quickly. Carlos, can you put these bones in dishes? Let's find out how many dishes of five bones can we draw to see how many days we can feed Paco.

Carlos encircles five bones.

Ms. Lo Cicero: Carlos, choose a friend to draw the next dish.

Finally three dishes are drawn.

Ms. Lo Cicero: So how many groups of five bones do we have here? Show me with your fingers.

Most students show three fingers.

Ms. Lo Cicero: So we have three dishes and how many bones are not in a plate?

Most students show two fingers.

Ms. Lo Cicero: So we have three *groups* of five and two *extra* bones. So how many do we have here?

Many students say 17.

Ms. Lo Cicero: Now we are going to think about things that have many parts. One thing with parts that look alike. In *one* hand, how many fingers do we have?

Many students say five, but some students don't know.

Ms. Lo Cicero: Remember to show me the answer with your fingers. Don't look at other students. Take your time. *(The teacher does this to practice numbers on fingers and to keep children from hearing the answer from the fastest child.)*

Ms. Lo Cicero *(showing a picture of a bicycle)*: In this *one* bicycle, how many wheels do we have?

Most students show two fingers.

Ms. Lo Cicero *(showing a picture of a tricycle)*: And in this *one* tricycle, how many wheels?

Most students show three fingers.

Ms. Lo Cicero: Who can give me examples of how one thing has many parts? These parts have to look the same. Look around the classroom.

Viviana: One chair has four legs.

Ms. Lo Cicero: Good thinking. Who can find in the classroom something else with four legs?

Carlos: The tables.

Ms. Lo Cicero: That is right. One table has four legs. Who can think of another thing that has four parts that are the same?

Luis: A wagon has four wheels.

Ms. Lo Cicero: What kind of wagon?

Luis: A train wagon.

Ms. Lo Cicero: Can you come and draw the train?

Luis draws a rectangle with four wheels below it.

Ms. Lo Cicero: Now let's talk about the number eight. Yesterday we talked about finding seven of something. Does anyone know what has eight parts that belong to one thing?

Edgar: Some trucks have eight wheels.

Ms. Lo Cicero: Very good!

Daniela: I know one! A spider has eight legs.

Ms. Lo Cicero: Any more groups of eight or eight parts?

Nanci: Two train wagons would have eight wheels. I'll show you. *(She draws another rectangle with four wheels beside Luis's wagon.)*

Already children are building on the contributions of others. The teacher has worked hard in the beginning to structure participation so that it requires hearing and making sense of what other children say and do, not just listening to or talking to the teacher.

Ms. Lo Cicero: Do you know what comes in front of the train? *(Silence)*

By asking questions the teacher discovers that not one student knows the Spanish or English word for engine *(locomotora)*, so she discusses that word in both languages. Building vocabulary is a natural and important aspect of this approach.

Ms. Lo Cicero: Let's pretend that we are going to check the wheels to see that everything is right. The mechanic has to check all eight wheels. Let's see, Linda, can you come and check the wheels?

She extends this fantasy situation to use one-to-one correspondence to show a how-many-more situation. Linda comes up front.

Ms. Lo Cicero: Check a wheel. *(Linda does nothing.)* Just pretend.

Several boys offer to help.

Ms. Lo Cicero: Linda can do it. Just see if the wheel is working. Once you check it, put a line under the wheel. *(Linda puts a line under the first wheel, gestures toward each of the next two wheels and draws lines under them.)* Linda, wait a minute before you continue checking. Class, Linda has to check eight wheels. She has checked three so far. How many more does she need to check? Show me with your fingers.

Many students show five.

Ms. Lo Cicero: Linda, count how many more you need to check to show everyone.

Linda: One, two, three, four, five. Five more.

Ms. Lo Cicero: Now check one more.

Linda: Now I have checked four.

Ms. Lo Cicero: She has to check eight in all. How many more does she need to check?

Most students show four fingers.

This checking and asking process continues through eight and zero. This scenario grew from the children's stories and was spontaneously co-invented by the teacher and the class. For example, Nanci used Luis's train wagon idea to respond to the teacher's request about eight. This class provided children experience with decomposing the number eight and with *how many more* language in a repeated context so that children can begin to make sense of the words *how many more* (which some children do not yet differentiate from the words *how many*).

The Next Day

Ms. Lo Cicero: Now let's pretend that you have a garden with many flowers and that your mother asks you to cut eight flowers and put them in two vases, one for the dining table and one for the TV. So let's draw the eight flowers. *(She draws them on the board.)* Let's see. Cinthia, how would you put some flowers in one vase and some in another vase?

Cinthia circles five flowers and the remaining three flowers.

The teacher goes on to have children do various decompositions of eight and begin to write numbers beside each decomposition. Each child then draws a pattern of eight circles and decomposes this pattern into various numbers "hiding inside eight."

Two Days Later

The teacher has children work with a partner to show pairs of numbers hiding inside ten. Children will do many activities so that the pairs to ten become very fast. They need to know these combinations to do adding and subtracting using ten. The first step in solving eight plus five by using ten is knowing that eight plus two is ten. Then they need to be able to break five into two plus three; decompositions of numbers help with this. Finally, they need to know that ten plus three is thirteen.

Fourth Week of School

Classes for the past week have been split between posing and solving simple word problems and decomposition activities. Since school began, children have done many activities concerning decomposition of ten and of smaller numbers on their fingers. For many days they have drawn all the decompositions they could think of for a number as homework, using their own patterns for numbers and horizontal rows of circles. Children have engaged in these activities at their own levels, but all are doing more advanced or more thorough approaches than at the beginning. By now many are beginning to memorize some of the combinations. Children have made various observations about some patterns in decompositions throughout this work. In this discussion the teacher is trying to enable them to express and reflect on many of these observations. Most children are still drawing groups of circles and circling them and then recording their numbers, but some children are working just with numbers.

Ms. Lo Cicero: Class, today we're going to discuss your homework. Let's talk about the numbers you found that made ten. You've been working with ten for a long time. Let's see how many different things we can say about the numbers in ten. Look at the board. Let's write some of your work. Who found a pair with one? Carlos? Tell me what you know.

Carlos: One and nine are inside ten.

Ms. Lo Cicero draws a row of ten circles.

Ms. Lo Cicero: Carlos told me he had one *(shades the first circle)*. Then there are nine left *(counts the rest)*: one, two, three, four, five, six, seven, eight, nine *(writes 1 and 9 to the right of the row)*. Who else?

Mrs. Lo Cicero elicits until she has all pairs. Children give these in various orders but she draws and shades them on the board in order from zero plus ten to one plus nine to two plus eight and so on, to eight plus two to nine plus one to ten plus zero. She leaves spaces for the missing ones to be reported and drawn.

Ms. Lo Cicero: Can someone tell me if they see something interesting here? [In English we ask, "Do you see a pattern?" In Spanish there is not a word for "pattern," so you have to talk around this concept.]

The teacher points to children to share what they see.

Andrés: If the first number is small, the other is big.

Marta: Eight and two is ten. Two and eight is also ten.

Viviana: That's true of other numbers. There's one and nine, and nine and one, and three and seven, and seven and three.

Roberto: And four and six, and six and four.

Jorge: But there's only one five and five.

Rufina: Ten plus zero is ten. And zero and ten are ten. Zero plus a number is the number. Zero doesn't add anything.

Karina: The numbers on the left go zero, one, two, three, four, five, six, seven, eight, nine, and on the right it is the opposite.

Josué: Numbers on the left get bigger by one and on the right they get smaller by one.

Jorge: I can make one row from another. I know six and four make ten, and one more is seven. So the other number is one less so it is three.

Ms. Lo Cicero: You are really getting good at noticing things and saying them so other children can understand you. In math it is really important to notice things. There are lots of interesting things in math. Now let's tell a math story and see what problems we can make from it.

Mid October

The class moves from the general grouping activities to focus more heavily on groupings of ten. This begins a series of activities supporting children's construction of a connected web of different meanings for two-digit numbers. All children initially count objects by ones, but they gradually build understandings of two-digit numbers as groups of ten and loose ones (53 is five groups of ten and three loose ones) and as sequence counting words (53 is made by counting by tens five times: 10, 20, 30, 40, 50, and then by counting on three more: 51, 52, 53).

Ms. Lo Cicero: Remember how we have been talking about groups: a group of two, a group of six, a group of five. Today we will make groups of ten. Groups of ten are especially important because our numbers use groups of ten. Also our money uses groups of ten. Today we are going to make groups of ten with pennies. We are going to find out how many groups of ten pennies we have. I will show you with my pennies, then you will do the same with your pennies. We are going to use a special worksheet and these penny strips to help us collect ten pennies. On each strip you can put ten pennies *(each strip has pictures of ten pennies with a space between the two groups of five so children can see eight as five plus three or six as five plus one).* We are learning to count pennies in a special way. We can also count other things in this way. We can count seeds, beans, or little stones. We will be working for many days learning to count money and to write it down. After we learn how to count money, we will be able to go to the market. Remember I told you we will learn about money so we can buy bones for Paco's dog and we can buy other things.

Ms. Lo Cicero grabs a bunch of pennies and goes around showing them.

Ms. Lo Cicero: Try to guess how many *groups* of ten pennies I have in my hands. In your worksheet you have the word *estimate*; that is like guessing but you think before you guess. Write down your *estimate* of how many *groups* of ten I have. *(Pause)* Now we'll find out. Teacher puts a penny strip on the board. *(Figure 10–1 shows ways in which children in a later lesson showed 53 with penny strips. One side of each strip has ten pennies with a space to show the five and five and the other side shows a dime.)* We will use this penny strip to help us see when we have ten. I will put my pennies on top of the pennies on this strip. How many pennies are on this strip? Let's count together. One, two, three, four, five, six, seven, eight, nine, ten. So there are ten pennies here. When I cover all of these pennies on the strip I will have ten pennies, *one group* of ten and *no* pennies extra, *no* loose pennies. When pennies are not in a group of ten, we say they are the loose ones, or that they are the extra ones. So let's see how many groups of ten I have and how many loose ones I have. How many *strips* can I fill? We will find out how many *groups* of ten I have and how many *loose* ones. Count with me.

The teacher begins filling the strip and counting as she sticks each penny on top of the penny on the strip.

STUDENTS: One, two, three, four, five, six, seven, eight, nine, ten.

MS. LO CICERO: So I have one ten, one *group* of ten, so far. Let's see if I can make another ten. *(She puts up another strip.)* Let's count together.

STUDENTS: One, two, three, four, five, six, seven, eight, nine, ten.

MS. LO CICERO: Yes! How many tens do I have?

STUDENTS: Two tens. 20.

MS. LO CICERO: How do you know we have 20?

VIVIANA: Because ten and ten is 20.

MS. LO CICERO: So how many *groups* of ten do I have?

STUDENTS: Two.

MS. LO CICERO: So I have two *groups* of ten and 10, 20 *(she points to each strip)* pennies. How many loose ones? Let's see. *(She puts up pennies.)* One, two, three, four. Do I have enough to make a ten?

STUDENTS: No.

MS. LO CICERO: So how many groups of ten?

STUDENTS: Two.

MS. LO CICERO: How many loose ones?

STUDENTS: Four.

MS. LO CICERO: That's right.

JUAN: You have 24 pennies.

MS. LO CICERO: How do you know that?

JUAN: Because 10, 20, 21, 22, 23, 24.

MS. LO CICERO: That is right. I have 10 *(gesturing across whole first strip)*, 20 *(gesturing across whole second strip)*, 21, 22, 23, 24 *(pointing to each penny)*. Twenty-four pennies. That makes one, two *(pointing to each strip)*—two *groups of ten* and *four loose ones,* four ones extra *(pointing to four pennies)*. Let's count them by ones just to make sure *(the class counts all of the pennies by ones as Ms. Lo Cicero points to each penny)*. Juan was right. We have 24 pennies, *two* groups of ten *(pointing to the two strips and writing the numeral 2 under the two strips)* and *four* loose ones, *four* ones extra *(writing the numeral 4 under the four pennies)*. We write *two* groups of ten, one, two *(pointing to each strip and then to the numeral 2)* in the tens place here on the left, and we write *four* loose ones, one, two, three, four *(pointing to each penny and then to the numeral 4)* in the ones place here on the right. Now I will give you some pennies, and I will help you do the same. Then we are going to learn to draw the pennies and write the number. There's a special way to write numbers bigger than nine. It uses these groups of ten.

Late November

The children have done penny strips and other grouping activities for three of the last six weeks. They were working on word problems and graphing (reading graphs that compare two quantities and making word problems from them) most of the rest of the time. Different children have constructed different parts of the two-digit web of meanings. Most can now count to 100 by ones and by tens because many activities focused on doing this in a meaningful way (e.g., discussing the structure of the English or Spanish number words and how the *ty* in *forty* or the *enta* in *cuarenta* means tens, so *forty* means *four tens*; putting up a finger as you say each ten and using the fingers to help you generate the next ten if you get stuck). Some children tend to emphasize the number words; they do many activities by counting by tens and ones. Others focus more on the written numbers and see them as so many groups of tens and loose ones. The activities are designed to help everyone build both kinds of meaning and eventually connect all of these meanings. Some children are still struggling with left-right issues, and so sometimes reverse the tens' and ones' position. Some children still prefer to count by ones.

Ms. Lo Cicero: Today, first make 53 using your penny strips.

She writes 53 on the board. Children work individually. (All of these methods are shown in Figure 10–1.)

Ms. Lo Cicero: How did you do it, Rosa? Come to the front and show us.

Rosa uses the large strips and pennies that stick on the chalkboard.

Rosa: I made five strips and three ones. See, 10, 20, 30, 40, 50 *(she points to each strip)*, 51, 52, 53 *(pointing to her three loose pennies)*.

Ms. Lo Cicero: Did anyone do it a different way? Moisés?

Moisés: One, two, three, four, five tens *(he counts as he puts up each strip)*, and one, two, three *(counting each penny as he puts it up)*. I knew 53 has five tens and three ones.

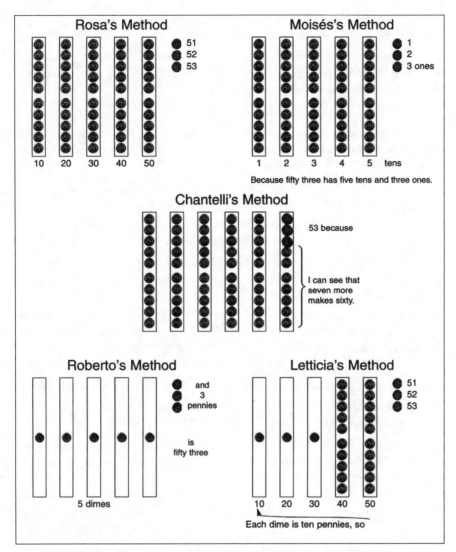

10–1 *Methods of making and counting 53 with penny strips*

Ms. Lo Cicero: Did anyone do something different? Chantelli?

Chantelli: I put my three pennies on another ten strip *(putting up six penny strips and puts three loose pennies on top of the three pennies at the top of the strip)*. So I can see how much more to 60 *(pointing to the penny pictures without pennies covering them)*. See, seven. Two more and five is seven.

Ms. Lo Cicero: So you can see that 53 *(gesturing to all coins on strips)* needs seven more to make 60 *(gesturing to printed pennies on last strip not covered by actual pennies)*. Anyone else?

Roberto: With 53 pennies we have five dimes and three pennies. *(His five strips show the dime side, and he puts up three pennies.)*

Ms. Lo Cicero: How did you know that?

Roberto: Each group of ten pennies is a dime *(he holds up a penny strip and shows the ten pennies and then the dime on the back)*, so 53 is five dimes and three pennies. We have 53 cents.

Ms. Lo Cicero: Class, did you all listen to how Roberto made his 53? Who can tell me what Roberto said just now? Carlos.

Carlos: He said he made 53 with five dimes and three pennies. That's like five groups of ten and three loose ones.

Ms. Lo Cicero: Yes, you're saying that Roberto's way is kind of like how Moisés did it by counting the tens because one dime is one group of ten pennies. Anyone else? Letticia.

Letticia: I used dimes *and* groups of ten pennies. I had three dimes *(she puts up three strips showing the dime side)* and two groups of ten pennies *(putting up two strips showing the penny side)* to make five tens and then three loose pennies *(putting up three pennies)*.

Ms. Lo Cicero: Can you show us how you know it makes 53 pennies?

Letticia: Each dime is ten pennies, so 10, 20, 30 *(pointing to each dime)*, 40, 50 *(pointing to each ten-penny strip)*, 51, 52, 53 *(pointing to each penny)*.

Ms. Lo Cicero: OK. That's kind of a hard way. Does everyone understand how Letticia's way works? Gabriela, can you come show us again? We'll help you if you need help.

Gabriela: 10, 20, 30, 31 *(first tens strip)*, 32 *(second tens strip)*, 33, 34, 35 *(she shifts to counting the pennies on the penny strip by ones but only counts each strip of ten once as 31, 32 instead of counting all of the pennies by ones)*.

Letticia: There are *ten* pennies here *(pointing to the first strip of pennies)*. You have to count all ten or say 40. You can't just count it 31.

Gabriela: 10, 20, 30 *(counting the 3 dimes by tens and then shifts to counting all the pennies on the penny strips by ones)*, 31, 32, 33, 34, 35, 36, 37, 38, 39, 40, 41, 42, 43, 44, 45, 46, 47, 48, 49, 50, 51, 52, 53. *(She prefers to think of the pennies as ones instead of counting two different kinds of tens.)*

Ms. Lo Cicero: Good counting, Gabriela. Can someone count it the other way Letticia said? Count this as *one* group of ten *(gesturing to first strip of pennies)*? Pedro, come write the numbers for us while you count.

Pedro comes and counts and writes the numbers as he counts.

PEDRO: 10, 20, 30 *(three dime strips)*, 40, 50 *(two ten-penny strips)*, 60, 70, 80 *(the three loose pennies). (He succeeds in counting each penny strip by ten but then keeps counting by tens when he counts the loose pennies, a typical early error. Some children initially find it hard to shift from counting by tens to counting by ones.)*

MS. LO CICERO: Are these loose pennies tens?

PEDRO: Oh, no.

MS. LO CICERO: So how do we count?

PEDRO: 10, 20, 30, 40, 50, 51, 52, 53.

MS. LO CICERO: Can you count again and count the groups of tens?

PEDRO: One group of ten, two groups of ten, three groups of ten, four groups of ten, five groups of ten, and one, two, three loose ones.

MS. LO CICERO: Very nice. So this 53 *(gesturing to the 53)* is *five* groups of ten *(gesturing to the 5 in 53 and then to the five strips)* and *three* loose ones *(gesturing to the 3 in 53 and the three loose pennies)*, *five tens (gesturing to the 5)* and *three ones (gesturing to the 3)* is 53. As Roberto said, we have 53 cents. (Teacher connects the quantities, words, and written numerals.)

May, First Grade

The children have been solving situations requiring the addition of two-digit numbers with regrouping on and off since late February. These problems were the first problems introduced so that from the beginning children would think about whether they get another ten in such situations. Children used the penny strips or drawn recordings of the strips in which a vertical line is a ten-penny strip and dots or circles are the loose pennies.

Most children can successfully solve and explain such problems if they use drawn quantities. Through such activities, many children are still constructing or automatizing their sequence meanings of number words (10, 20, 30, . . .) or their meanings of two-digit written numbers as groups of tens and loose ones (48 as four groups of ten and eight loose ones). Some children are still having trouble remembering whether the tens are on the left or on the right. New children who have entered the class since January missed a lot of the early quantity work and some are still behind, though the teacher has been trying to organize extra help for them to catch up. Some children do so quickly, and others more slowly.

Today the teacher is beginning the reflective process of shifting children from methods using objects or drawn quantities (penny strips and pennies or drawn ten-sticks and dots) to methods relying on mental versions of the operations on physical or drawn quantities. In inventing these mental methods, children use their meanings for two-digit numbers. Some children use sequence meanings and methods (count by tens), some use collected-tens methods (count the tens), and some use a combination, shifting flexibly between these kinds of meanings. Between a third and a half of the children are not yet ready; they still need to use drawn quantities. In the second grade many children will need to fall back to using drawn quantities when they encounter new and difficult problems.

MS. LO CICERO: Can you discover a way to add all the tens and all the ones without having to draw them all and count them all? Try it for this problem.

She writes 49 + 25 horizontally. The children work independently and sometimes in consultation with each other or the teacher.

MS. LO CICERO: OK, let's see some of the ways you have discovered. Nanci.

The methods are shown in Figure 10–2. Nanci comes to the blackboard. She looks at the tens (the four and the two) and explains.

NANCI: A four and a two in my mind.

MS. LO CICERO: Two what?

NANCI: Four tens and two tens.

Nanci writes a 6, looks at the ones, erases the 6.

NANCI: I can make another ten, and then you count the ones and it's . . . *(Pauses, counts five fingers onto nine, writes 74.)*

MS. LO CICERO: Can you tell us how?

NANCI: Nine, and another ten *(first finger of the five more)* is seven tens, and one, two, three, four *(putting up four new fingers for the rest of the 5)* is 74.

Nanci has invented a precursor to the look-ahead method widely taught in Europe. In this method you start on the left, add a column, look ahead to see if you're getting another ten and increase your total if you are, write the tens, then add the next column (to the right) in the

Nanci's Method

49 + 25 = 6

Four tens and two tens (writes 6).
(Looks at the ones; erases the 6.)
I can make another ten, and then you count
the ones (fingers count 5 on to 9), writes 74.

Later she invents a way to record the new ten:

$$\overset{3}{49 + \cancel{2}5} = 74$$

Cinthia's Method

25 + 47

I took three from the five and put it with the
seven. Then I counted two plus four is six.
Then there is another ten, so seven tens,
and there are two left, seventy-two.

Later she invents

$$\overset{5}{48 + 2\cancel{7}} = 75$$

Viviana's Method

48 + 23

Forty and two tens makes sixty.
Eight in my mind. 68, 9, 10, 11, 71.

Martha and Rufina's Methods

$$\overset{1}{\underline{3}7 + \underline{2}6} = 63$$

$$\underset{\underline{48 + 16}}{} = 64$$

$$\begin{array}{r} \overset{1}{25} \\ + \ 49 \\ \hline \end{array}$$

Jorge's Method

56 + 27 =

I know these are tens.
50, 60, 70. Then I counted 7 (7 fingers up):
71, 72, 73, 74, 75, 76, 77. Then I counted 6
more (6 fingers up): 78, 79, 80, 81, 82, 83.

Karina's Method

37 + 56

Eight. / Eighty seven
(counts on fingers, 6 fingers)
8, 9, 10, 90, 93

Methods of Marking Tens and Ones

TO   TO
34 + 19 = __ __

4|8 + 1|6 = __ __

$\underline{4}$7 + $\underline{2}$8 = __ __

25 + 47 = __ __

10–2 Mental and written numeric two-digit addition methods

same way. This method generalizes to problems with large numbers and
can be done meaningfully. Most children's methods work from left to
right.

The teacher then asks the class to try to figure out other ways to add
all the tens and ones together without having to draw them all and count
them all. The teacher gives some more problems to experiment on and
tours the class while they do. This first phase gives the teacher direct

feedback on where the children are, what they're ready for, and what sort of help they'll need. Most important, there usually are some children, from the very beginning, with productive invented methods. This further reinforces the general orientation of the class toward inventive problem solving because the invention is focused upon and credited to the inventor.

Ms. Lo Cicero: Now let's have some more children explain their discovery of how to add without drawing and counting all of the ten-sticks and ones. Jorge has a good method. Jorge, come explain what you discovered.

The problem is 56 + 27 written horizontally. Jorge has invented a mental counting-on method for the tens; he then puts up fingers for the ones and counts them on from the tens' total. He uses the written form of the problem on the board to point out what he was grouping orally and with his fingers.

Jorge: I know these are tens *(pointing to the 56 and 27)*, 50, 60, 70. Then I counted seven *(putting up one hand and two fingers and then counts them)* 71, 72, 73, 74, 75, 76, 77. Then I counted six more *(putting up one hand and one finger and then counts them)* 78, 79, 80, 81, 82, 83.

Two other children's hands shoot up, and they volunteer that they do it like that as well. Juan describes his method and does it pretty much like Jorge. But Viviana shows a way to collapse the counting on of the initial ones from the tens (she chooses to explain 48 + 23).

Viviana: Forty and two tens makes 60. Eight in my mind. 68 *(she just adds the 8 to 60)*, 9, 10, 11 *(she counts these three without using her fingers)*, 71.

Ms. Lo Cicero: Can you explain how you got the 71?

Viviana: Forty and two tens makes 60. Eight in my mind. 68, 69, 70, 71.

The teacher asks the class to try it Jorge's, Juan's, and Viviana's way. About half the class does, and the rest continue doing it the way they had been. This is fine. At this stage many still need to operate by drawing and counting all the quantities. The suggestion to "Try it ___'s way" is best thought of as an invitation for those who feel ready to try that method.

In this class, about one-third of the class immediately invent a wide range of correct and efficient methods, another one-third struggle in various ways over several days to figure out some way not to lose track of the extra ten (in contexts where they no longer have it present before them in the form of drawn ones counted and regrouped into a ten), and about one-third at first prefer to continue drawing and counting all the tens and ones, as they had been doing.

Over the next several days, the focus is on various inventors showing the class their ways of solving regrouping problems mentally and numerically. The class tries out sóme of these ways. Small groups of the children who are struggling toward workable methods work together and compare their approaches, usually with some help from the teacher sometime during a class period.

The Next Day

While the teacher is touring the class observing problem solving, she notices that Cinthia and Karina have each invented a ten-structured method, splitting the ones into the part needed to make a ten and the ones remaining. Cinthia solves the problem and explains 25 + 47 like this: "I took three from the five and put it with the seven. Then I counted two plus four is six. Then there is another ten *(this shows she is thinking of the two plus four equals six as tens)*, so seven tens, and there is two left. 72." Karina starts from the tens first, on the problem 37 + 56. She points at the tens numbers 3 and 5 while saying, "Eight, *(then points at the 7 in 37)* 87, *(points at the 6 in 56 and counts on her fingers)* 8, 9, 10, 90 *(80 plus that 10 was really 90)*, 93 *(chunking the three from the six over 90)*."

Next Several Days

The children in the bottom third of the class have been struggling unsuccessfully with remembering the extra ten when solving without drawn quantities. Some add the tens first, and some add the ones first. Sometimes these children remember the extra ten, sometimes not. Many of them also have trouble with what turns out to be one of the main underlying problems when numbers are written horizontally: sorting out which are the tens and the ones. Giving problems vertically right away may allow children to work without really understanding tens and ones. The teacher gathers the strugglers together into a group to see what they can figure out among themselves (and with teacher help) that would be effective. Pedro, having begun to learn the traditional carry method from home, lobbies for it as a reminder of the extra ten. Everyone in the group agrees that this is a good way to do things, but when they begin to work on their own, most immediately start to do quite different things. Martha and Rufina break into a working pair of their own and devise three different ways (see Figure 10–2): underlining tens when using the horizontal equation form, making loops that connect tens' places in one number to tens in the other number, or (in the vertical case) vertical lines from tens to tens. Martha prefers to store the extra ten mentally, Rufina by writing it, but by the end of this session both make errors less frequently. Linda sometimes stores mentally, sometimes with a carry mark, but also from this point on, rarely makes mistakes. Pedro, noticing that few were following the carry procedure, attempts to lobby for it more, but no one pays attention, so he goes back to working on his own. Gabriela and Luis get the main attention of the teacher because they are having trouble consistently. Across several sessions Gabriela steadily becomes more accurate in remembering an extra ten. Luis consistently needs to rewrite a horizontal equation in vertical form, and he uses a carry procedure only partially understood at that time.

During these days, Nanci and Cinthia go on to invent symbolic numeric supports for their methods (see Figure 10–2). These might be especially helpful as they move to larger numbers where the mental load of remembering everything is greater. Later in first grade and in second grade, many of the children still drawing and counting tens and ones can only shift to numeric or mental methods when they visually mark which are the tens and which are the ones as Martha and Rufina do, or in the other ways shown in Figure 10–2. They can distinguish tens from ones and use these when they are visually clear as with drawn ten-sticks and ones, but need some kind of written support when only using numbers because the numbers just look like single digits.

December, Second Grade

Ms. Lo Cicero: We have been talking about money all year. We studied the value of our coins. We talked about some of your experiences in buying and selling. We learned how to give change from a dime and from a quarter. We used the penny strips, and now we are using money. Remember we acted out Mercado [a small store] and worked in pairs. Today we will learn to give change from a dollar. We need to help everyone learn to give change before we can have our bake sale. I will pass you each a bag [sandwich bag] containing coins. Fold a sheet of paper in four equal parts. Draw different ways of making up one dollar.

Students work for ten minutes. Some converse and help each other. The teacher observes methods and asks questions of students to find out their thinking, or to help them understand, describe, or correct their method, or to see if a child is ready to move on to a more advanced method.

Ms. Lo Cicero: Now imagine that you are buying a pencil that costs 37 cents. How much change will you get back? You may draw, write down numbers, or use ten-sticks and dots. I want to see how you work this out. Try different ways. Remember how we drew the coins before.

Students work for twenty minutes. The teacher goes around checking and helping the students. She is also looking for good examples that later may be used by the whole class and for typical errors that may need to be discussed.

Ms. Lo Cicero: Let's have Juan come up and show his way. Draw your first dollar. Juan, explain what you did in your first drawing. [See Figure 10–3.]

Juan: I drew ten dimes. Ten dimes make one dollar. 63 is the answer.

Ms. Lo Cicero: Can you explain what you did with this dime?

Juan: One dime has ten pennies, or a nickel and five pennies. I took 37, and now I have 63.

Ms. Lo Cicero: You took 37 from what? From how much?

Juan: From one dollar.

Ms. Lo Cicero: How do you know you have a dollar?

Juan: Ten dimes is the same as one dollar.

Ms. Lo Cicero: How many cents do you have in one dollar?

Juan: 100.

Ms. Lo Cicero: Who else would like to show their way? Viviana, yes, you may come. Let's see, show us the second solution *(looking at her paper)*.

Viviana: Shall I draw it? [See Figure 10–3.]

Ms. Lo Cicero: Yes, please. Tell us how you thought about all this.

Viviana: 25 plus 10 is 35 plus 2 *(pointing to her underlined coins)* is 37. Then I counted what I had left: 25 plus 25 is 50 plus 10 is 60 plus 3 is 63.

Ms. Lo Cicero: Good thinking! Who would like to show another way?

Chantelli: These tens *(the ten-stick drawings of the penny strips)* are my dimes [see Figure 10–3]. There's three left in this dime *(pointing to the split ten-stick)* and six more dimes.

Ms. Lo Cicero: Can you count up to give me change with this money here?

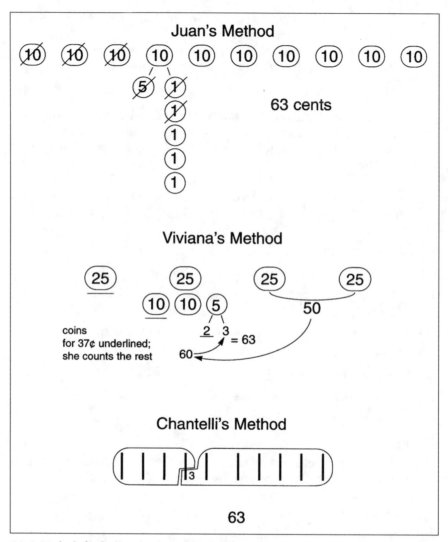

10–3 Methods for finding the change for $.37 from $1.00

CHANTELLI: Here is three pennies to make 40 cents, and 60 more is one dollar. Here is 10, 20, 30, 40, 50, 60.

MS. LO CICERO: Very nice. You found lots of ways to show how you give change from a dollar. Tomorrow we will do Mercado [children work in pairs buying and selling] and practice giving change from a dollar for our bake sale. [Such practice is important because counting up with money is more difficult for children than counting up with penny strips or ten-sticks, because the money does not look like tens—the dimes are even smaller than the pennies.]

January, Second Grade

The class is working on problems comparing heights. They are using inches so that the heights will be two-digit numbers. Later they will use centimeters to get three-digit numbers. They have been finding the difference in height between Jorge and Cinthia's little brother Paulo: 62" and 37". They also are working on different ways to ask the difference questions. Here several students explain how they solved the problem. (See Figure 10–4.)

GABRIELA: *(She has drawn three dots, then two ten-sticks, then two dots, and written 25; the other numbers are what she says in her explanation.)* I said, "How much does Paulo have to grow?" so 37 plus 3 more *(pointing to three dots)* is 38, 39, 40, and 50 *(pointing to a ten-stick)*, 60 *(pointing to another ten-stick)*, 61, 62 *(pointing to the two dots)*. So this is 23 *(gesturing to the three dots and two ten-sticks)*, 24, 25 more he has to grow to catch Jorge.

ROBERTO: I shrunk the big guy down by taking away the little guy from him *(gesturing to his drawing of the little guy beside the big guy and the line he drew across from the top of the little guy to the big guy)*. So 62 minus 37 is 25 [see Figure 10–4]. I took three tens from the six tens and seven from this ten. That leaves three and these two are five and two tens left is 25.

MS. LO CICERO: I am going to ask someone to tell me how Josué explains it. You all need to listen to him. I know it is really hot in here today *(the heating system in the building malfunctions, and the room is stifling; some children had put their heads down and were not watching)*. Let's all take five big deep breaths before Josué explains so we can all concentrate. Ready, ooooone, twoooooo, threeeeeeee, fouuuuuurrrrr, fiiiiivvvvve. Good. Josué.

JOSUÉ: I did it like Gabriela but I wrote three and then my ten-sticks and two and then added them to get 25 more the little guy needs. [See Figure 10–4.]

MS. LO CICERO: Karina, how did Josué do it?

KARINA: Like Gabriela but he used numbers and sticks.

MS. LO CICERO: What did he start with?

KARINA: 37 and made 25 more.

MS. LO CICERO: Can someone else say in their words how Josué did it?

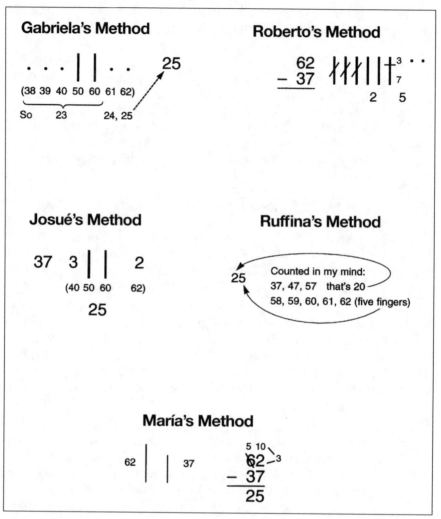

Gabriela's Method

. . . | | . .   25

(38 39 40 50 60 61 62)

So   23   24, 25

Roberto's Method

$$\frac{62}{-37}$$ | | | | | | ³ . .
                           ⁷
               2   5

Josué's Method

37 3 | | 2

(40 50 60   62)

25

Ruffina's Method

25   Counted in my mind:
      37, 47, 57   that's 20
      58, 59, 60, 61, 62 (five fingers)

María's Method

62 | | 37   5 10
                 62⁻³
              − 37
              ‾‾‾‾
                25

10–4 Methods for finding the difference in height between 62 inches and 37 inches

NANCI: He used numbers and sticks to go 37 plus 3 is 40 plus 2 tens is 60 plus 2 to get to Jorge. So 2 tens and 5 is 25.

MS. LO CICERO: OK. Ruffina.

RUFFINA *(She has just written 25 above her little guy drawing, [see Figure 10–4]):* I just counted in my mind 37, 47, 57, that's 20 *(she points to the 2 in 25),* then 58, 59, 60, 61, 62 *(raises five fingers as she counts),* so that's 5. 25.

MARÍA: I subtracted Paulo from Jorge like Roberto did, but I used numbers. I took one of the tens to get enough to take away the seven, so that was three and two more was five ones, and there were two tens left so 25.

MS. LO CICERO: Can someone else tell how Roberto's and María's methods are alike?

CARLOS: They both took away the little guy to get the difference. They took away 37 from 62.

MS. LO CICERO: Anything else?

JAZMIN: They both had to open a ten because there weren't seven ones to take away. So Roberto took his seven from that ten-stick. *(Teacher points to show the ten-stick Roberto separated into seven and three, and looks questioningly at Jazmin.)* Yes, there he took seven and left three. And María took a ten from the six tens and wrote it with the ones and then took the seven to leave three. *(Teacher points to the top right part of María's problem.)*

MS. LO CICERO: So they were both thinking about taking ones from a ten but they wrote it in different ways?

SEVERAL STUDENTS: Yes.

LETTICIA: And we know other ways to write subtraction, too.

MS. LO CICERO: Yes, you have lots of ways you show taking away and comparing, too. Whose heights should we compare next?

Discussion

Tasks

This chapter contains many examples of tasks that children problematized: decomposing numbers, searching for patterns in the decomposed pairs, different ways of showing 53, adding multidigit numbers, finding 49 + 25 without drawing objects, making change, and finding differences in heights. Initially, children contributed to generating mathematical situations and contexts that were familiar, and the teacher supported them in learning to mathematize these situations. As the children's mathematical thinking developed, their thinking, and the various methods children devised, increasingly became the focus of classroom discussions. Over time, children took increasing responsibility for the ideas discussed and for helping their classmates in their mathematical thinking.

In order to make mathematics problematic, teachers need to select tasks that are accessible to children but are not already automatic. However, sometimes the teacher needs to do activities to help children make certain things automatic. For example, after children understand and have drawn decompositions to ten for some period of time, Ms. Lo Cicero had children practice these so that they would be available for mental ten-structured methods of adding and subtracting. Children also practiced counting by tens: This must be automatic if children are to use addition or subtraction methods involving counting by tens. Children regularly do distributed practice on homework: They have a range of problems they have done earlier as well as the current problems. But most of the tasks done in class are ones that are problematic for many students. Helping other children solve a problem in their own way can also be problematic and can extend the helper's mathematical thinking because of the new perspective.

Role of the Teacher

A vital new role is to understand children's thinking about mathematics. Teachers have told us that one of the most exciting things about changing from a traditional mathematics classroom to teaching mathematics with understanding is that the teacher constantly has a chance to learn more about children's thinking and about mathematics itself. The teacher no longer has to be the sole authority, but can participate with children in figuring out some mathematical situation. Our teachers say that they would never go back to teaching in the old ways. Earlier, neither they nor most of their children understood some or even much of the mathematics that was being taught and learned. Understanding mathematics, and looking forward to understanding even more about mathematics and about children's mathematical thinking, is now a vital and energizing part of our teachers' professional self-image. This attitude and the feeling of involvement and self-confidence that it generates enable classrooms to be exciting and interesting places for children and for teachers.

Once a teacher experiences a year focusing on children's thinking, she or he is in a position to have a vision of progressions in children's thinking and various solution methods children use. This enables the teacher to set learning goals throughout the year for children who are progressing at different speeds and to select tasks and tools that support children through these learning goals. In the examples here, Ms. Lo Cicero used (with the introduction of the penny strips) the different kinds of language she knew that the children would need to carry out different addition and subtraction methods. She talked about groups of ten so that children could understand the meaning of the tens' place. She counted these tens as tens (one, two groups of ten) and also as sequence counting words (10, 20), thus relating these two meanings. She counted by ones, the counting that all children could do, to relate these new ways of thinking to children's present ways of thinking and present skills. She repeatedly used all forms of language and linked these to the quantities (the strips and loose pennies) and to the written numerals so that children could begin to build quantity meaning for the numerals. Later, some children used each of the kinds of language she had introduced: Some used methods in which they thought of units of ten and counted tens (Moisés, Nanci, and Roberto), and other children counted by sequence tens (Rosa, Viviana, and Gabriela).

The penny strips are also an example of another vital role of the teacher: to share essential mathematical information and to design activities to help children understand this information. The penny strips were introduced to help children understand the value of money and to help children build quantity meanings for written two-digit numerals. Both money and written place value are arbitrary mathematical or social-cultural conventions that the teacher must help children come to understand.

Classroom Culture

Ms. Lo Cicero consciously worked to establish a classroom culture in which children felt safe and confident enough to share their thinking. Many children, especially those who do not come from middle-class backgrounds, need models of the desired kinds of classroom discourse; they are not used to talking about their thinking. Some of our children had never been in a school classroom of any kind before first grade. The early examples show how a teacher might get started involving children in classroom discussions. Ms. Lo Cicero did a great deal of talking in these early episodes. She was doing many different things: building a class feeling, modeling how children might talk, helping children describe their thinking, ensuring that children speak loudly enough for their classmates to hear, keeping children involved, focusing attention, and helping children learn to listen to their classmates. She was very patient with children and waited for the long time it sometimes took them to find words, while gently offering encouragement if needed. She constantly began with some situation that was familiar to many of the children, mathematized that situation with respect to her mathematical goals at the time (which might necessitate changing some aspect of the situation), and then wove that mathematical thinking back to the situation. She tried to create coherence and continuity over many days by returning to earlier situations and extending them to new mathematical topics.

As children build the desired mathematical concepts and methods, they come to be able to take over more and more of the discussion. The later examples demonstrate that the teacher can now elicit methods from many children without helping them to clarify nearly as much as was necessary earlier. Some children have become quite sophisticated about seeing methods that are similar, even if there are differences in the methods (e.g., Jorge, Juan, and Viviana for their invented two-digit addition methods; Karina in describing Gabriela's and Josué's methods of finding the difference in heights). Children even take over some of the teacher's initial roles, such as helping others understand (e.g., Letticia explaining to Gabriela when Gabriela counts a tens strip by ones instead of tens). This cycle of teacher modeling and greater support will need to be carried out again whenever a class enters a mathematical domain in which considerable new knowledge must be constructed. As one of our first-grade teachers summarized this process at a recent meeting for other teachers, "It is a great deal of work at the beginning to build the classroom environment you need. But then the children just take over and do it mostly themselves. And it is so wonderful to see what they can do then!"

Tools as Learning Supports

The figures all show tools children learned to use to support their mathematical thinking and their communication about their thinking. These tools became quantitatively meaningful for individual children through activities in which they counted, added, and subtracted the quantities in the tools. The penny strips and the earliest forms of the drawn ten-sticks (ten dots or short horizontal dashes with or without a line drawn through them) allowed children to carry out the most primitive methods, counting by ones. Classroom activities during this time helped children build the more advanced views of these tools as supporting sequence counting methods or methods counting groups of tens by ones. In all of these activities, the quantities were linked to written numerals and to spoken number words (both the sequence counting words and the tens and ones words). The drawn ten-sticks and dots enabled children to write numbers beside them to clarify the meanings and the method used. Such linking supported reflection by children on their own methods, and it facilitated communication to others about that solution method. Children followed discussions of other children's thinking better if that child or the teacher pointed to objects or numbers during the description of the method. Having children work at the board or on individual blackboards was one way to have the child's work visible as they explained. The examples given in the figures show how the tools, and the numbers themselves, could and did take on different meanings for different children. These meanings were supported by activities using the tools in the classroom.

Equity and Accessibility

Our project uses activities that can be solved in multiple ways ranging from the more primitive to the more advanced so that all children can participate. Acceptance of such a range of methods is important, as is monitoring by a teacher of students' readiness to move on to a more advanced method. Teachers often directly support such moving on by activities in which everyone tries a given method (e.g., the class tried Jorge's, Juan's, and Viviana's method of two-digit addition) and with tutoring with adults or peers. Helping children use the most advanced method of which they are capable at a given time, while not undermining their autonomy or confidence, is an important aspect of equity for us. It is also important to try to make such help available for children who cannot initially do even the simplest method in a given domain.

Supporting nontraditional gender roles in mathematical thinking is also valuable. The teacher needs to monitor whether she or he is enabling girls to participate as capably and as frequently as do boys. A classroom climate of all learners as teachers, and of all children as responsible for their classmates, can also increase equity and access to mathematical thinking with understanding. We have found that all children can progress substantially in their mathematical thinking, in their confidence and clarity in describing their thinking, and in their helping behavior.

11 Revisiting the Critical Features of Classrooms

The previous four chapters provide glimpses into classrooms that illustrate, in somewhat different ways, the system of instruction that we outlined in Chapters 1–6. By showing classrooms in action, they bring to life the features of classrooms that we think are essential. By showing the various forms this system of instruction can take, they help us sort out what is essential and what is optional.

In this chapter, we look back at the five dimensions that make up the system we recommend, and we draw examples from the classrooms to review the features within each dimension that are critical. Along the way, we point to some features that are optional, features that can distract attention away from the things that really matter.

The chapter will follow the outline suggested in Figure 1–1, and readers may want to refer back to this figure as we look at each dimension.

Nature of Classroom Tasks

There are three features of classroom tasks that are critical: First, the situation must be one that students can treat problematically. The tasks cannot just be exercises on which students are suppose to practice a prescribed procedure. Second, the tasks need to connect to something the students know and are able to do. Students must have some tools available that allow them to begin working out methods for solving the problem. Third, what is problematic about the task should be the mathematics of the situation so that what gets left behind is something of mathematical value. The first two features work closely together so we will review them together.

Tasks That Students Can Problematize and That Are Within Reach
We noted near the end of Chapter 4 and in Chapter 6 that whether students problematize a task will depend as much on the culture of the

classroom as on the task itself, but the task must at least afford students the chance of treating it as a genuine problem. This means there must be something to work out, some quandary to resolve, and students have some skills and tools with which they can begin to solve the problem.

In Chapter 7, Ms. Keith allowed students to shape the tasks in ways that would fit these requirements. After presenting the two tasks for the day, she asked the students what they should do "If the numbers are too big?" The students responded that they should change them to "Numbers that are challenging." The fact that first and second graders were able to do just that indicates that, if appropriate expectations are developed, students can problematize tasks, even to the point of tailoring them to their own levels. In other words, even young students can understand what it means to treat mathematics as problematic.

Tasks that are selected by the teacher, without adjustments by the students, can also fit the requirements. Finding the missing item in the lunch at a fast-food restaurant (Chapter 8), the number of apple tarts that could be made from 20 apples (Chapter 9), and the difference between the heights of Jorge and Paulo (Chapter 10) were challenging—but not impossible—tasks for the students in each of these classrooms. Teachers chose these tasks because they connected to skills and tools that students already possessed and, at the same time, they provided room for the students to treat them problematically and generate their own solution methods.

Tasks That Leave Residue of Mathematical Value

When tasks are chosen so the mathematics of the situation is what becomes problematic, then the task is likely to leave something behind of mathematical value. In Ms. Keith's classroom (Chapter 7), Vicki tried to solve the problem $123 + 456 - 98$. She used several different methods, got different answers, and solicited help from Roger. Roger pointed out some technical problems but Vicki was not satisfied. She had defined the problem for herself as one of working out three different methods, all of which should generate the same answer. She was committed enough to this problem that she wanted to share her developments with Ms. Keith, even though it meant giving up recess time. Through the process of resolving her mathematical problems, she constructed new insights into how numbers could be decomposed and recombined, insights that were likely to remain with Vicki long after she forgot the solution to the problem.

Whether or not tasks leave behind something of mathematical value does not depend on how they are packaged—whether they are large-scale, real-life projects, clever puzzles, or simple, unadorned tasks. What matters is that, as students engage the tasks, they reflect on mathematical relationships and ideas.

Role of the Teacher

The four previous chapters show teachers playing very different roles, from managing and directing whole class discussions (Chapters 8 and 10) to allowing students to work on different problems and engaging in individual conversations with students (Chapter 7) to withdrawing from the scene temporarily and allowing students to work (Chapter 9). Despite these rather obvious differences, there are some features that all the classrooms shared.

Select Tasks with Goals in Mind

The teachers in these classrooms viewed the selection of sequences of tasks as the primary way in which they could guide the curriculum and increase the likelihood that students would take with them particular mathematical residues. Perhaps this is seen most clearly in Chapter 10, where Ms. Lo Cicero carefully selected tasks from the beginning of first grade through second grade that encouraged students to construct mathematical relationships that built on each other over time. In other words, later tasks connected with the residues that were likely to have been left by earlier tasks.

An up-close view of this selection process is provided in Chapter 8. Ms. Devon adjusted slightly the numbers in the calorie counts for some menu items so that students would need to think about how to handle a variety of regrouping situations. Ms. Devon's intent was for students to adjust their old methods or invent new ones and, in doing so, to construct additional insights into the structure of the number system.

Although the selection of sequences of tasks does not require wildly creative or clever ideas, it does require careful thought about the mathematics landscape and about the way in which a series of tasks might lead students across the landscape. As described in Chapter 3, this is a challenging responsibility, and it is a responsibility that the teachers in these classrooms took seriously.

There are different routes across the landscape. All teachers do not need to choose the same tasks or sequences or follow the same curriculum plan. Our experience suggests there are many options for the selection and sequencing of tasks. For example, students in Ms. Devon's classroom (Chapter 8) worked on place value tasks before they added and subtracted multidigit numbers, whereas students in Ms. Keith's classroom (Chapter 7) did not encounter special place value tasks but engaged place value ideas while they added and subtracted multidigit numbers. Students in both classrooms constructed important insights into the base-ten number system and developed appropriate solution methods for a variety of problems. Different paths can be used to reach similar goals. What is important is that the teacher selects sets of tasks that connect with where students are and that lead toward the learning goals the teacher envisions.

Share Information

How much information to share, and what kind of information to provide, are dilemmas with which teachers must continually struggle. We noted in Chapter 3 that teachers will need to share mathematical conventions, such as vocabulary and notation, and may wish to suggest alternative solution methods and articulate important ideas contained within students' methods. The classroom episodes in the previous chapters show teachers suggesting notations and words that might help students express their methods, and rephrasing students' methods to draw attention to important ideas, but never demonstrating solution methods that students should use.

For example, Ms. Keith (Chapter 7) suggested tree diagrams and arrow notation as ways that students could record their solution methods. These informal conventions helped students keep track of their work and helped them remember what they had done when they shared their methods with the class. Ms. Lo Cicero (Chapter 10) responded to Pedro's count of 53 using penny strips in November of first grade, by reiterating pieces of his method that showed the connections between the groupings of objects, the words, and the written symbols. She elaborated Pedro's method to underscore an important connection, a connection to which she wanted students to attend.

One of the reasons that the teachers in these episodes did not suggest solution methods was that they believed students were capable of inventing their own methods, borrowing methods from their peers, and refining their methods as they had more opportunities to solve problems. Our experience suggests that this is the case throughout the primary grades. As students move through the middle grades and beyond, and the mathematics becomes increasingly complex and increasingly dependent on mathematical conventions, teachers may wish to share solution methods for the class to consider. There is nothing wrong with this if students do not believe they should mimic the method just because the teacher presented it. As we said in Chapter 3, the bottom line is why students choose a particular method. Students should use methods because they understand them and can defend them, not because they feel obligated to use them or to please the teacher. Methods should be preferred *based on their merits*, not based on who presented them.

Upper elementary + middle School dilemma

Guide the Development of the Culture

There are many things a teacher can do to lead the students in developing a classroom culture in which reflection and communication are valued. We highlighted two of these in Chapter 3: A teacher can focus the discussions on methods of solution, and allow the correctness of the solution to come from the logic of the mathematics rather than from the word of the teacher. The preceding chapters contain multiple instances of teachers' actions that are consistent with these features.

Ms. Keith (Chapter 7) demonstrated repeatedly her interest in the students' methods by the way in which she listened to students. Listening carefully to descriptions of methods sends a powerful signal to students that methods are to be respected. The conversations in this classroom also indicated that students did not depend on the teacher to correct their solutions or methods. Vicki got two answers to the same problem, said "I can't seem to find what I did wrong," and then consulted with Roger on the potential flaws in her methods. Vicki felt that it was her responsibility to work out the correctness of her solutions and to track down errors in her methods.

Chapter 9 shows what can happen when an inquiry culture has been established. Students can take control of tasks, problematize them, focus their attention on developing appropriate methods, and decide on correctness by the persuasiveness of the mathematical argument. Chapter 10 shows one way such cultures might develop. Over a two-year period, students were given increasing responsibility for introducing the important mathematical ideas into the conversation. At the beginning of first grade, the teacher carefully structured the discussions and scaffolded students' contributions; by the middle of second grade, students were providing the kind of elaborated descriptions and explanations that made such scaffolding unnecessary.

By comparing the classrooms portrayed in Chapters 7 and 10, one can see that there are different ways in which teachers can guide the development of an appropriate classroom culture. Ms. Keith took a less active role in directing and scaffolding the activities and discussions of students than Ms. Lo Cicero. In one classroom students were working in a variety of grouping arrangements; in the other classroom students were working as a whole class. We believe that these differences in the way the classrooms were managed and the students were grouped are optional features of classroom culture. Teachers can choose a style with which they feel most comfortable. What is essential, and what these teachers shared, is that they were working toward the goal of establishing a classroom culture in which reflection on, and communication about, mathematics were highly valued.

Social Culture of the Classroom

We have just reflected on the role of the teacher in establishing an appropriate culture in the classroom. Now we will look a little further into the attributes of such a culture.

Ideas and Methods Are Valued

One of the most striking things about the classroom episodes in the four previous chapters is that almost all of the classroom conversations were about methods students used to solve problems. A task was presented, usually by the teacher, and then a considerable amount of time was devoted to students' presentations of methods, questions and comments about methods, analysis of methods, comparisons of methods, and so on. In these classrooms, the mathematics happened in the methods. Doing mathematics meant developing, explaining, reflecting on, and improving methods: Mathematical concepts and procedures were acquired, and mathematical relationships were constructed through the process of developing and improving methods for solving problems.

The collaborative effort of four girls solving the apple tart problem (Chapter 9) illustrates that doing mathematics begins when the method for solving the problem becomes the central issue. When other issues dominate the social culture (as during the first part of the girls' collaboration), students cannot really do mathematics. But when they focus on the method of solution, serious reflection and communication about mathematics can begin.

Students Choose and Share Methods

Students, rather than the teacher, should choose the methods they use and share with the class. It is essential that students have autonomy over which method they choose, but it is optional whether they use a method they have invented or one they have borrowed from another student or the teacher. Recall that in Ms. Devon's classroom (Chapter 8) many students used the standard algorithm for subtracting multidigit numbers. Some students had learned the method at home and shared it with the class, and the teacher directed students' attention to the method and how it connected with actions on the base-ten blocks. In contrast, many students in the other classrooms used other methods to subtract. In all the classrooms, which methods students chose was up to them. What is essential is that the social culture of the class encourage open discussion of methods and that students know they can choose methods they understand.

Sharing methods is also essential. As noted near the end of Chapter 9, the episode of solving the apple tart problem illustrated how important it is for each student to be able to describe his or her method. Putting our own ideas into words is a powerful teacher. We understand better when we have the opportunity to describe and explain our thinking. But sharing does more than help our own understanding. The social culture of the classrooms that we have described views sharing as the responsibility of each student to help his or her classmates understand. In fact, as noted in Chapter 4, it is useful to think of understanding in the following way: A person understands when he or she can communicate in a way that helps others understand. Even young students can establish a culture with this feature. Recall Angela's observation after she described her addition procedure for 263 + 149 that began with combining the hundreds: "I think that would have been a lot easier to explain if I had started at the other end" (Chapter 8). Angela was taking responsibility for sharing a method in a way that others could understand and benefit.

Mistakes Are Learning Sites

A major difficulty for teachers who are beginning to use the system of instruction we are describing is how to handle the errors that inevitably occur when students develop their own solution methods. In addition to rereading the relevant sections in Chapter 4, the most helpful suggestion we can provide is to think again about the way in which classroom teachers actually dealt with the errors that occurred in the previous episodes.

Three examples illustrate three important points. When Ms. Keith asked Diana about her solution and method (Chapter 7), the conversation centered around the nature of the method that was used. Diana was interested in improving her method, and her classmates chimed in with suggestions about methods that might work better. The mistakes were viewed as methods that could be improved. Viewing mistakes in this way allows them to become useful starting points rather than dead ends.

When Ms. Devon asked how someone might have generated the (incorrect) solution 232 (Chapter 8), Adam eagerly volunteered that he knew because that was his answer. Adam explained his thinking and Ms. Devon used the chance to discuss a common misconception. These students had developed a culture in which errors were viewed as potentially useful points of discussion and they were more than willing to explain their errors and contribute to such discussions.

When Ms. Lombard allowed the four girls to continue working on their own despite the errors they were making (Chapter 9), they eventually corrected many of their errors. The students understood that they were responsible for developing appropriate solution methods and for checking the correctness of their work. In fact, it is reasonable to think that the benefits of this activity for the students came, in part, because Ms. Lombard did not interfere and so the students needed to find ways to correct their own work.

These examples show that errors can be viewed, by teachers and students, in constructive ways. A social culture can be developed in which errors are not embarrassing signs of stupidity but are natural and constructive consequences of building improved methods of solving problems. Examining errors and thinking about how they arise can be viewed as essential components of classroom discussions that are making progress toward understanding.

Correctness Resides in Mathematical Arguments

We have already described the teacher's role in allowing students to use the analysis of methods and the mathematical merits of arguments to determine correctness, and we have pointed back to examples which show that students can accept this responsibility. We have found that, if the tasks are appropriately challenging for students and if students have had time to work out their best solutions, teachers can reflect solutions back to students for discussion and rely on them to sort out the arguments and determine correctness.

To underscore the importance of this feature, we can reconsider the episode of solving the apple tart problem (Chapter 9). Earlier we said that the fourth graders began engaging in serious mathematics when they problematized the task and made it their own. Another way to say the same thing is that this occurred when they took responsibility for determining the correctness of their solutions. For the first part of the episode, the students exchanged answers and even shared methods. But they were not really committed to solving the problem. They had reached an impasse because different answers were suggested and they had not yet committed themselves to resolving their disagreements. When one of the students suggested drawing the apples, and the others bought into this idea, they began a new phase in their work. One could say they had problematized the task. One could also say they had accepted the responsibility to determine the correctness of the solution through the development of mathematical arguments that they all could understand.

Mathematical Tools as Learning Supports

Doing mathematics requires the use of tools. Although tools include more than physical materials, we will review several examples with materials to revisit the major points.

Students Must Construct Meaning for Tools

If tools are to be used to reflect on mathematics and communicate about mathematics, rather than as just mechanical aids or answer-getting devices, students must have opportunities, over time, to construct meaning for them. Consider the experiences of students in Ms. Lo Cicero's classroom (Chapter 10) in developing meaning for the pennies and penny strips to show ones and tens. Students began building meaning for the tool in first grade when they arranged pennies in groups of ten. As the meaning for the tool developed, the tool became increasingly useful for adding and subtracting multidigit numbers. The payoff of having a tool like this available is seen in the January episode of second grade, when several students used the tool to develop creative methods for solving a subtraction problem. Students' descriptions of their methods made it clear that they were using the tool to think about the ideas, not just to generate an answer. This is what tools can do if students have been allowed and encouraged to develop meaning for them.

Tools Must Be Used for a Purpose

As we noted in Chapter 5, tools in everyday life are always used for some purpose, to accomplish something, to complete a task. The same should be true for mathematical tools in the classroom. In all of the instances of tool use in the previous chapters, the purpose was to solve problems. Sometimes teachers asked students to use particular tools, other times students could choose which tools to use. But tools were always used to solve problems. This is true for the base-ten blocks, the tree diagrams, the arrow notation, and the counting frame in Chapter 7, the base-ten blocks in Chapter 8, the drawings of apples in Chapter 9, and the fingers and penny-strips in Chapter 10. Which tools, and how many, to introduce into the classroom is optional. What is essential is that students are given opportunities to develop meaning for tools and to use them to solve problems.

Tools Should Be Used to Record, Communicate, and Think About Mathematics

As teachers think about which tools to introduce, they should consider the ways in which the tools could help students solve problems by recording their ideas and methods, communicating these to others, and reflecting on the mathematical ideas. A number of examples from the previous chapters show the choices these teachers made.

Ms. Keith (Chapter 7) introduced the arrow notation and tree diagrams for recording and communicating solution methods. Figures 7–3, 7–4, 7–6, and 7–7 show that students were able to use these tools effectively. Ms. Lo Cicero (Chapter 10) introduced pennies and penny-strips for ones and tens and later encouraged students to draw facsimiles of these objects. Figures 10–1 and 10–4 show that students used this tool effectively. Of course, students can also develop their own tools, as did the fourth graders (Chapter 9) who drew pictures of apples and partitioned them.

As students use tools to record and communicate, they also use the tools to guide their thinking. Andrew's (Chapter 8) description of how he subtracted 273 from 501 shows one way in which this happens. He had written the problem on paper and looked at the numbers and was momentarily stuck: "I knew I needed a ten but there weren't any and then I thought about the blocks and then I knew what to do." Andrew had worked with the base-ten blocks for some time and now seemed to use his mental images of them to guide his thinking. Used in this way, tools can be powerful aids for solving problems.

Equity and Accessibility

An integral part of the system of instruction that we have described is the full participation of all the students in the class. As we noted in Chapter 6, this requires the teacher to be vigilant in creating a classroom that invites and values each student's participation. This means that the tasks must be accessible, in some form, to all students, that the norms of the classroom culture include listening carefully to each student, and that the classroom environment enable each student to contribute.

Tasks Must Be Accessible to All Students

Earlier we noted that different teachers used different ways of ensuring that the tasks were accessible to each student in the class. Ms. Keith (Chapter 7) asked students to adjust the numbers so the task was problematic but within reach. The other teachers expected the students to work with the task that was presented but were careful in selecting tasks that connected with students' current ways of thinking and the tools that were available.

The teachers in these classrooms were also careful to select contexts for tasks that were reasonably familiar to students and, in some cases, contexts in which students were highly interested. For example, all the students in Ms. Devon's class (Chapter 8) had been to fast-food restaurants and she knew from informal conversations that they enjoyed eating at these places. Because of this, she periodically embedded problems in these contexts. It is important to remember, however, that, although an interesting context may support students' engagement, it does not make the mathematics of the situation accessible. Teachers must think carefully about accessibility, not just about context.

Our primary concern with context is that the context for a task should not be so unfamiliar for some students that it places them at a disadvantage when they try to interpret the situation and treat it as a mathematical problem. The contexts of problems should not favor some students over others.

Every Student Must Be Heard

Listening is an essential feature of the social culture of classrooms and an essential feature of equitable learning environments. Not all students can learn if only some students are heard. Teachers play a major role in creating classroom cultures with listening norms. In fact, listening carefully to each student is one of the most powerful ways they can model appropriate behavior and guide the development of the culture.

What it means to listen can be described by recalling several instances from the previous classroom episodes. When students were working (Chapter 7), Ms. Keith circulated around the room and talked with individual students. But she did not move quickly from student to student. She spent considerable time listening to each of them. Even when she understood Karen's strategy partway through the description, she listened carefully to Karen's complete explanation. It may be easy for teachers to listen if a student is saying something new or intriguing, but it is just as important for teachers to listen when they are quite certain what they will hear.

Listening also means trying to understand what the speaker means. If a student offers a comment that is not easy to follow, it can be tempting to pretend it is understood and move on. This is one way to promote inequity because it leads quickly to shutting some students out of the conversation. Listening means taking the time to work out what each speaker intends to say. There are many instances in Chapters 7, 8, and 10 of teachers modeling this kind of listening, and the episode in Chapter 9 shows that students can share this behavior.

A third aspect of listening is respecting the ideas that are offered. Teachers can model this by treating each contribution as a learning opportunity. One way in which this can happen is to follow the implications of the students' observations. When Angela (Chapter 8) said "I think that would have been a lot easier to explain if I had started at the other end," Ms. Devon seized the opportunity, reflected Angela's observation back to the class, and coordinated a discussion on the advantages of different methods. By taking Angela's observation seriously, she demonstrated that listening means more than just passive acceptance; it means pursuing the ideas that have been offered. This is one of the surest signs of respect.

Every Student Must Contribute

We noted near the end of Chapter 9 that the episode of solving the apple tart problem showed how important it was for each of the four students to express their ideas in words that others could understand. We said that the exchanges between the students illustrated the strong need students have to clarify their own thinking by putting it into words. This message is dramatized most forcefully in Chapter 9 because we hear the same students over an extended period of time, but we believe it was true for students in the other classrooms as well. Every student needs an opportunity to articulate their ideas, and the teachers in these classrooms were conscious of this need.

An implication of this feature is that every student must feel that they have something to contribute. In most cases, this means that they must have the support and encouragement they need to develop solution methods they understand. Two examples help to make this point: Diana (Chapter 7) was struggling to develop more advanced strategies for adding 18 + 23 + 37, and Ms. Keith encouraged her to work on alternative methods, but did not require her to abandon the more primitive strategies she understood. This allowed Diana to always have available a method she understood, a method she could share.

A second example comes from looking across the years in Ms. Lo Cicero's class (Chapter 10). By carefully selecting a sequence of tasks involving multidigit numbers, the students were able to build on what they had done earlier, always retaining a connection to what they understood from previous work. Although not all the students were working at the same level, the selection of tasks and the culture of the classroom afforded them the chance to share their methods, to put their thinking into words.

Conclusions

We began this book with the premise that understanding is the most fundamental goal of mathematics instruction, the goal upon which all others depend. We then asked "What kinds of classrooms facilitate mathematical understanding?" Our primary aim throughout this book has been to provide the most complete and useful answer that is currently available.

We used two methods to describe classrooms that facilitate understanding: The first was to outline the crucial dimensions that must be considered when building classrooms for understanding (Chapters 1–6). Within each dimension, there are some features that we believe are essential and some that are optional. The essential features are intertwined and work together to create classrooms for understanding. They define a system of instruction rather than a series of individual components. It makes little sense to introduce a few of the features and ignore the rest; their benefits come from working together as a coherent, integrated system.

The second way in which we described classrooms that facilitate understanding was to present actual episodes from classrooms. The aim was to provide a glimpse of how the system of instruction we outlined in theory can work in practice. The pictures from different classrooms make it clear that the system of instruction we describe is not a prescription or a step-by-step method of teaching, but rather a tightly connected set of principles that identify critical features of instruction. Although these features work closely together, they can be shaped by teachers into a variety of forms. The classrooms we described show teachers taking ownership of the system, honoring its essential principles, and making somewhat different choices about features that are optional.

Teachers are professionals: Not only are they responsible for choosing the system of instruction they will develop but also for making the day-to-day decisions about the way in which they will implement the system. We hope that this book has provided a context within which teachers can reflect on their practice, think about the system of instruction they are using, and consider changes they would like to make. We hope, in addition, that teachers, and all those concerned with the educational process, will consider seriously the system of instruction we have described and will use the classroom episodes to envision how the system can be implemented in mathematics classrooms.

Notes

Chapter 6
Equity and Accessibility

1. The research reported in this chapter was supported in part by a grant from the National Science Foundation (MDR-8955346) and by the National Center for Research in Mathematical Sciences Education, which is funded by the Office of Educational Research and Improvement of the U.S. Department of Education under Grant No. R117G10002. The opinions expressed in this chapter are those of the authors and do not necessarily reflect the views of NSF or OERI.

   We are grateful to Mazie Jenkins and Susan Gehn for allowing us to visit and report on their classrooms.

Chapter 7
A Day in the Life of One Cognitively Guided Instruction Classroom

1. The research reported in this chapter was supported in part by a grant from the National Science Foundation (MDR-8955346) and by the National Center for Research in Mathematical Sciences Education, which is funded by the Office of Educational Research and Improvement of the U. S. Department of Education under Grant No. R117G10002. The opinions expressed in the chapter are those of the authors and do not necessarily reflect the views of NSF or OERI.

   We are grateful to Ellen Ansell and Stephanie Smith for the significant contributions they made to this chapter. Ellen Ansell spent two years studying Annie Keith's classroom. Her observations and insights played a critical role in the preparation of the chapter. The description of the classroom episode is based on a videotape of a mathematics lesson in Ms. Keith's class filmed by Stephanie Smith. Her thoughtful orchestration of the filming made it possible for us to portray critical aspects of children's learning and the classroom context that supported that learning.

2. The children call the counting frame an abacus, but it differs from the Chinese abacus in that there are ten beads in each row, and the children use each row to represent a collection of ten rather than to represent place value (see Figure 7–5).

3. The protocols are verbatim transcriptions from a video of the class. Students' written work has been copied from the video to represent as accurately as possible the critical features of their solutions.

4. Ms. Keith learned about buggy algorithms in an inservice workshop, and she introduced the term to her class. They picked up on the term, and both Ms. Keith and the students often refer to errors in procedures as "bugs."

Chapter 8
A Day in the Life of a Conceptually Based Instruction Classroom

1. The study in which Ms. Devon's class participated was funded by a grant from the National Science Foundation (Grant No. MDR-8855627). We would like to thank the many teachers and students who made this project possible by allowing us to implement alternative instruction in their classrooms and to observe them teach and learn.

Chapter 10
Snapshots Across Two Years in the Life of an Urban Latino Classroom

1. The research reported in this chapter was supported in part by the National Center for Research in Mathematical Sciences Education, which is funded by the Office of Educational Research and Improvement of the U.S. Department of Education under Grant No. R117G10002, in part by the National Science Foundation under Grant No. RED 935373, and in part by the Spencer Foundation. The opinions expressed in this chapter are those of the authors and do not necessarily reflect the views of OERI, NSF, or Spencer. Correspondence concerning this article should be addressed to Karen C. Fuson, School of Education and Social Policy, Northwestern University, 2115 N. Campus Drive, Evanston, Illinois 60208–2610. Electronic mail may be sent via Internet to fuson@nwu.edu.

   This paper reflects the work of the whole *Children's Math Worlds* team and the extraordinary support of the teachers with whom we worked: Sara Avelar, Elba Cora, Myrna Nunez, Mary Olsen, Jennifer Tozer, and Mary Westphal. Ana Lo Cicero, Steven T. Smith, and Kristin Hudson co-authored this chapter with Karen Fuson.

References

AAUW Report. 1992. *How Schools Shortchange Girls*. Washington, DC: Author.

Ansell, E. 1995. *Understanding Children's Strategy Use as Classroom Activity*. Unpublished doctoral dissertation, University of Wisconsin, Madison, WI.

Ball, D. L. 1993a. "Halves, Pieces, and Twoths: Constructing and Using Representational Contexts in Teaching Fractions." In *Rational Numbers: An Integration of Research*, ed. T. P. Carpenter, E. Fennema, and T. A. Romberg, 157–95. Hillsdale, NJ: Erlbaum.

———. 1993b. "With an Eye on the Mathematical Horizon: Dilemmas of Teaching Elementary School Mathematics." *Elementary School Journal* 93: 373–97.

Bebout, H. C. 1990. "Children's Symbolic Representation of Addition and Subtraction Word Problems." *Journal for Research in Mathematics Education* 21: 123–31.

Brownell, W. A. 1947. "The Place of Meaning in the Teaching of Arithmetic." *Elementary School Journal* 47: 256–65.

———. 1946. "Introduction: Purpose and Scope of the Yearbook." In *Forty-Fifth Yearbook of the National Society for the Study of Education: Part I. The Measurement of Understanding*, ed. N. B. Henry, 1–6. Chicago: University of Chicago.

———. 1935. "Psychological Considerations in the Learning and Teaching of Arithmetic." In *The Teaching of Arithmetic. Tenth Yearbook of the National Council of Teachers of Mathematics*, ed. W. D. Reeve, 1–31. New York: Teachers College Press.

Bruner, J. S. 1966. *Toward a Theory of Instruction*. New York: Norton.

————. 1960. *The Process of Education.* Cambridge, MA: Harvard University Press.

CAREY, D. A., E. FENNEMA, T. P. CARPENTER, and M. L. FRANKE. 1993. "Equity and Mathematics Education." In *New Directions in Equity for Mathematics Education,* ed. W. Secada, E. Fennema, and L. B. Adajian, 93–125. New York: Cambridge University Press.

CARPENTER, T. P., E. ANSELL, M. L. FRANKE, E. FENNEMA, and L. WEISBECK. 1993. "A Study of Kindergarten Children's Problem-Solving Processes." *Journal for Research in Mathematics Education* 24 (5): 428–41.

CARPENTER, T. P., and E. FENNEMA. 1992. "Cognitively Guided Instruction: Building on the Knowledge of Students and Teachers." *International Journal of Research in Education* 17 (5): 457–70.

CARPENTER, T. P., E. FENNEMA, and M. L. FRANKE. 1996. "Cognitively Guided Instruction: A Knowledge Base for Reform in Primary Mathematics Instruction." *Elementary School Journal* 97: 3–20.

CARPENTER, T. P., E. FENNEMA, P. L. PETERSON, C.P. CHIANG, and M. LOEF. 1989. "Using Knowledge of Children's Mathematical Thinking in Classroom Teaching: An Experimental Study." *American Educational Research Journal* 26: 499–531.

CARPENTER, T. P., and R. LEHRER. 1996. *Teaching and Learning Mathematics with Understanding.* Technical Report, National Center for Research in Mathematical Sciences Education, University of Wisconsin, Madison, WI.

CARPENTER, T. P., J. M. MOSER, and H. BEBOUT. 1988. "The Representation of Basic Addition and Subtraction Word Problems." *Journal for Research in Mathematics Education* 19: 345–57.

COBB, P., K. GRAVEMEIJER, E. YACKEL, K. MCCLAIN, and J. WHITENACK. In press. "Mathematizing and Symbolizing: The Emergence of Chains of Signification in One First-Grade Classroom." In *Situated Cognition Theory: Social, Semiotic, and Neurological Perspectives,* ed. D. Kirshner and J. A. Whitson. Hillsdale, NJ: Erlbaum.

COBB, P., T. WOOD, E. YACKEL, and B. MCNEAL. 1992. "Characteristics of Classroom Mathematics Traditions: An Interactional Analysis." *American Educational Research Journal* 29: 573–604.

COBB, P., T. WOOD, E. YACKEL, J. NICHOLLS, G. WHEATLEY, B. TRIGATTI, and M. PERLWITZ. 1991. "Assessment of a Problem-Centered Second-Grade Mathematics Project." *Journal for Research in Mathematics Education* 22: 3–29.

COLBURN, W. 1849. *Colburn's First Lessons. Intellectual Arithmetic Upon the Inductive Method of Instruction*. Boston, MA: William J. Reynolds.

———. 1837. *Colburn's First Lessons. Intellectual Arithmetic Upon the Inductive Method of Instruction*. Concord, NH: O.L. Sanford.

DAVIS, R. B. 1992. "Understanding 'Understanding'." *Journal of Mathematical Behavior* 11: 225–41.

DEWEY, J. 1933. *How We Think: A Restatement of the Relation of Reflective Thinking to the Educative Process*. Boston: Heath.

———. 1929. *The Quest for Certainty*. New York: Minton, Balch & Co.

———. 1910. *How We Think*. Boston: Heath.

DOISE, W., and G. MUGNY. 1984. *The Social Development of the Intellect*. New York: Pergamon.

DOYLE, W. 1988. "Work in Mathematics Classes: The Context of Students' Thinking During Instruction." *Educational Psychologist* 23: 167–80.

———. 1983. "Academic Work." *Review of Educational Research* 53: 159–99.

FENNEMA, E. 1990. "Justice, Equity, and Mathematics Education." In *Mathematics and Gender*, ed. E. Fennema and G. Leder, 1–10. New York: Teachers College Press.

FENNEMA, E., T. P. CARPENTER, and M. L. FRANKE. In press. "Knowledge Action Research and Cognitively Guided Instruction in Mathematics." In *Action Research and the Reform of Mathematics and Science Education*, ed. M. L. Watt.

FENNEMA, E., T. P. CARPENTER, M. L. FRANKE, L. LEVI, V. R. JACOBS, and S. B. EMPSON. 1996. "A Longitudinal Study of Learning to Use Children's Thinking in Mathematics Instruction." *Journal for Research in Mathematics Education* 27 (4): 403–34.

FENNEMA, E., M. L. FRANKE, T. P. CARPENTER, and D. A. CAREY. 1993. "Using Children's Mathematical Knowledge in Instruction." *American Educational Research Journal* 30 (3): 555–83.

———. 1992. "Learning to Use Children's Mathematical Thinking: A Case Study." In *Schools, Mathematics, and the World of Reality*, ed. R. Davis and C. Maher, 93–112. Needham Heights, MA: Allyn & Bacon.

FUSON, K. C. 1992. "Research on Learning and Teaching Addition and Subtraction of Whole Numbers." In *The Analysis of Arithmetic for Mathematics Teaching*, ed. G. Leinhardt, R. T. Putnam, and R. A. Hattrup, 53–187. Hillsdale, NJ: Erlbaum.

FUSON, K. C., and D. J. BRIARS. 1990. "Using a Base-Ten Blocks

Learning/Teaching Approach for First- and Second-Grade Place-Value and Multidigit Addition and Subtraction." *Journal for Research in Mathematics Education* 21: 180–206.

Fuson, K. C., J. L. Fraivillig, and B. H. Burghardt. 1992. "Relationships Children Construct Among English Number Words, Multiunit Base-Ten Blocks, and Written Multidigit Addition." In *The Nature and Orgins of Mathematical Skills*, ed. J. Campbell, 39–112. The Netherlands: Elsevier Science.

Fuson, K. C., and Y. Kwon. 1991. "Learning Addition and Subtraction: Effects of Number Words and Other Cultural Tools." In *Pathways to Number*, ed. J. Bideaud, C. Meljac, and J. P. Fischer, 283–302. Hillsdale, NJ: Erlbaum.

Fuson, K. C., D. Wearne, J. Hiebert, P. Human, H. Murray, A. Olivier, T. P. Carpenter, and E. Fennema. 1997. "Children's Conceptual Structures for Multidigit Numbers at Work in Addition and Subtraction." *Journal for Research in Mathematics Education* 28(2): 130–62.

Gates, B. 1995. *The Road Ahead.* New York: Viking Press.

Good, T. L., C. Mulryan, and M. McCaslin. 1992. "Grouping for Instruction in Mathematics: A Call for Programmatic Research on Small-Group Processes." In *Handbook of Research on Mathematics Teaching and Learning*, ed. D. A. Grouws, 165–96. New York: Macmillan.

Greeno, J. G. 1991. "Number Sense as Situated Knowing in a Conceptual Domain." *Journal for Research in Mathematics Education* 22: 170–218.

Hatano, G. 1988. "Social and Motivational Bases for Mathematical Understanding." In *Children's Mathematics*, ed. G. B. Saxe and M. Gearhart, 55–70. San Francisco: Jossey-Bass.

Hiebert, J. 1992. "Reflection and Communication: Cognitive Considerations in School Mathematics Reform." *International Journal of Educational Research* 17: 439–56.

———. 1990. "The Role of Routine Procedures in the Development of Mathematical Competence." In *Teaching and Learning Mathematics in the 1990s: 1990 NCTM Yearbook*, ed. T. J. Cooney, 31–40. Reston, VA: National Council of Teachers of Mathematics.

———. ed. 1986. *Conceptual and Procedural Knowledge: The Case of Mathematics.* Hillsdale, NJ: Erlbaum.

Hiebert, J., and T. P. Carpenter. 1992. "Learning and Teaching with Understanding." In *Handbook of Research on Mathematics Teaching and Learning*, ed. D. A. Grouws, 65– 97. New York: Macmillan.

Hiebert, J., T. P. Carpenter, E. Fennema, K. Fuson, P. Human, H. Murray, A. Olivier, and D. Wearne. 1996. "Problem Solving as a Basis for Reform in Curriculum and Instruction: The Case of Mathematics. *Educational Researcher* 25 (4): 12–21.

HIEBERT, J., and D. WEARNE. 1996. "Instruction, Understanding, and Skill in Multidigit Addition and Subtraction." *Cognition and Instruction* 14: 251–83.

———. 1993. "Instructional Tasks, Classroom Discourse, and Students' Learning in Second-Grade Arithmetic." *American Educational Research Journal* 30: 393–425.

———. 1992. "Links Between Teaching and Learning Place Value With Understanding in First Grade." *Journal for Research in Mathematics Education* 23: 98–122.

HIEBERT, J., D. WEARNE, and S. TABER. 1991. "Fourth Graders' Gradual Construction of Decimal Fractions During Instruction Using Different Physical Representations." *Elementary School Journal* 91: 321–41.

KAMII, C. 1985. *Young Children Reinvent Arithmetic*. New York: Teachers College Press.

KAMII, C., and L. L. JOSEPH. 1989. *Young Children Continue to Reinvent Arithmetic*. New York: Teachers College Press.

LAMON, S. 1995. "Ratio and Proportion: Elementary Didactical Phenomenology." In *Providing a Foundation for Teaching Mathematics in Middle Grades*, ed. J. T. Sowder and B. P. Schappelle. Albany, NY: State University of New York Press.

LAMPERT, M. In press. "Studying Teaching as a Thinking Practice." In *Thinking Practices*, ed. J. Greeno and S. G. Goldman. Hillsdale, NJ: Erlbaum.

———. 1991. "Connecting Mathematical Teaching and Learning." In *Integrating Research on Teaching and Learning Mathematics*, ed. E. Fennema, T. P. Carpenter, and S. J. Lamon, 121–52. Albany, NY: State University of New York Press.

———. 1985. "How do Teachers Manage to Teach?" *Harvard Educational Review* 55: 178–94.

LAMPERT, M., P. RITTENHOUSE, and C. CRUMBAUGH. In press. "Agreeing to Disagree: Developing Sociable Mathematical Discourse in School." In *Handbook of Psychology in Education*, ed. D. Olson and N. Torrance. Oxford: Blackwell.

MATHEMATICAL SCIENCES EDUCATION BOARD. 1988. *A Framework for Revision of the K–12 Mathematics Curriculum*. Washington, DC: National Research Council.

MCDONALD'S NUTRITION INFORMATION CENTER. 1996. *McDonald's Foods: The Facts*. Oak Brook, IL: McDonald's Corporation.

MCLAUGHLIN, M. W. M., and L. A. SHEPARD, with J. A. O'DAY. 1995.

Improving Education Through Standards-Based Education Reform. A Report by the National Academy of Education Panel on Standards-Based Education Reform. Stanford, CA: National Academy of Education.

MEANS, B., and M.S. KNAPP. 1991. "Introduction: Rethinking Teaching for Disadvantaged Students." In *Teaching Advanced Skills to At-Risk Students,* ed. B. Means, D. Chelemer, and M.S. Knapp, 1–26. San Francisco: Jossey-Bass.

MURRAY, H., A. OLIVIER, and P. HUMAN. 1993. "Voluntary Interaction Groups for Problem-Centered Learning." In *Proceedings of the Seventeenth PME Conference (Vol. 2),* ed. I. Hirabayashi, N. Nohda, K. Shigematsu, and F. Lin, 73–80. Tsukuba, Japan.

———. 1992. "The Development of Young Students' Division Strategies." In *Proceedings of the Sixteenth PME Conference (Vol. 2),* ed. W. Geeslin and K. Graham, 73–80. Durham, NH: University of New Hampshire.

NATIONAL ASSESSMENT OF EDUCATIONAL PROGRESS. 1983. *The Third National Mathematics Assessment: Results, Trends, and Issues.* Denver, CO: Education Commission of the States.

NATIONAL COUNCIL OF TEACHERS OF MATHEMATICS. 1995. *Assessment Standards for School Mathematics.* Reston, VA: National Council of Teachers of Mathematics.

———. 1991. *Professional Standards for Teaching Mathematics.* Reston, VA: National Council of Teachers of Mathematics.

———. 1989. *Curriculum and Evaluation Standards for School Mathematics.* Reston, VA: National Council of Teachers of Mathematics.

NODDINGS, N. 1985. "Small Groups as a Setting for Research on Mathematical Problem Solving." In *Teaching and Learning Mathematical Problem Solving: Multiple Research Perspectives,* ed. E. A. Silver, 345–59. Hillsdale, NJ: Erlbaum.

NATIONAL RESEARCH COUNCIL. 1989. *Everybody Counts: A Report to the Nation On the Future of Mathematical Education.* Washington, DC: National Academy Press.

PALEY, V. G. 1986. "On Listening to What the Children Say." *Harvard Educational Review* 56: 122–31.

PARKER, R. E. 1993. *Mathematical Power: Lessons from a Classroom.* Portsmouth, NH: Heinemann.

PIRIE, S., and T. KIEREN. 1994. "Growth in Mathematical Understanding: How Can We Characterize It and How Can We Represent It?" *Educational Studies in Mathematics* 26: 165-90.

PORTER, A.C. 1991. "Good Teaching of Worthwhile Mathematics to Disadvantaged Students." In *Better Schooling for the Children of Poverty: Alternatives to Conventional Wisdom*, ed. M. S. Knapp and P.M. Shields, 125–48. Berkeley, CA: McCutchan.

PUTNAM, R. T., M. LAMPERT, and P. L. PETERSON. 1990. "Alternative Perspectives on Knowing Mathematics in Elementary Schools." In *Review of Research in Education, Vol. 16*, ed. C. Cazden, 57–150. Washington, DC: American Educational Research Association.

QIN, Z., D. W. JOHNSON, and R. T. JOHNSON. 1995. "Cooperative Versus Competitive Efforts and Problem Solving." *Review of Educational Research* 65: 129–43.

RESNICK, L. B., and S. OMANSON. 1986. "Learning to Understand Arithmetic." In *Advances in Instructional Psychology (Vol. 3)*, ed. R. Glaser, 41–95. Hillsdale, NJ: Erlbaum.

SALOMON, G., and T. GLOBERSON. 1989. "When Teams Do Not Function the Way They Ought To." *International Journal of Educational Research* 13: 89–99.

SAXE, G. B., M. GEARHART, and V. DAWSON. 1996. "When Can Educational Reforms Make a Difference? The Influence of Curriculum and Teacher Professional Development Programs on Children's Understanding of Fractions." Manuscript.

SCHOENFELD, A. H. 1994. "What Do We Know About Mathematics Curricula?" *Journal of Mathematical Behavior* 13: 55–80.

———. 1989. "Ideas in the Air: Speculations on Small Group Learning, Environmental and Cultural Influences on Cognition and Epistemology." *International Journal of Educational Research* 13: 71–88.

SIMON, M. A. 1995. "Reconstructing Mathematics Pedagogy from a Constructivist Perspective." *Journal for Research in Mathematics Education* 26: 114–45.

SKEMP, R. R. 1987. "Relational Understanding and Instrumental Understanding." In *The Psychology of Learning Mathematics*, 152–63. Hillsdale, NJ: Erlbaum. (Reprinted from *Mathematics Teaching*, the Bulletin of the Association of Teachers of Mathematics, No. 77, December 1976.)

STEIN, M. K., and S. LANE. In press. "Instructional Tasks and the Development of Student Capacity to Think and Reason: An Analysis of the Relationship Between Teaching and Learning in a Reform Mathematics Project." *Educational Research and Evaluation*.

STEIN, M. K., B. W. GROVER, and M. HENNINGSEN. 1996. "Building Student Capacity for Mathematical Thinking and Reasoning: An Analysis of Mathematical Tasks Used in Reform Classrooms." *American Educational Research Journal*, 33: 455–88.

STIGLER, J. A., and M. PERRY. 1988. "Cross-Cultural Studies of Mathematics Teaching and Learning: Recent Findings and New Directions." In *Perspectives on Research on Effective Mathematics Teaching*, ed. D. A. Grouws and T. J. Cooney, 194–223. Reston, VA: National Council of Teachers of Mathematics.

VAN ENGEN, H. 1947. "Place Value and the Number System." In *Arithmetic 1947*, ed. G. T. Buswell, 59–73. Chicago, IL: The University of Chicago Press.

VYGOTSKY, L. S. 1978. *Mind in Society: The Development of Higher Psychological Processes*. ed. M. Cole, V. John-Steiner, S. Scribner, and E. Souberman. Cambridge, MA: Harvard University Press.

———. 1962. *Thought and Language*. Cambridge, MA: M.I.T. Press.

WEARNE, D., and J. HIEBERT. 1989. "Cognitive Changes During Conceptually Based Instruction on Decimal Fractions." *Journal of Educational Psychology* 81: 507–13.

———. 1988a. "A Cognitive Approach to Meaningful Mathematics Instruction: Testing a Local Theory Using Decimal Numbers." *Journal for Research in Mathematics Education* 19: 371–84.

———. 1988b. "Constructing and Using Meaning for Mathematical Symbols: The Case of Decimal Fractions." In *Number Concepts and Operations in the Middle Grades*, ed. J. Hiebert and M. Behr, 220–35. Reston, VA: National Council of Teachers of Mathematics.

WEBB, N. M., J. D. TROPER, and R. FALL. 1995. "Constructive Activity and Learning in Collaborative Small Groups." *Journal of Educational Psychology* 87: 406–23.

WHEAT, H. G. 1951. "The Nature and Sequences of Learning Activities in Arithmetic." In *The Fiftieth Yearbook of the National Society for the Study of Education, Part II: The Teaching of Arithmetic*, ed. G.T. Buswell, 22–52. Chicago, IL: The University of Chicago Press.

———. 1941. "A Theory of Instruction for the Middle Grades." In *Arithmetic in General Education: Sixteenth Yearbook of the National Council of Teachers of Mathematics*, ed. W. D. Reeve, 80–118. New York: Teachers College Press.

———. 1937. *The Psychology and Teaching of Arithmetic*. Boston: D.C. Heath.

WHITEHEAD, A. N. 1948. *An Introduction to Mathematics*. London: Oxford University Press.

MAKING SENSE